Mother, If in Heaven There Are No Apples, I Don't Want to Go There!

∽∾∾

Christel Decker Bresko

DORRANCE PUBLISHING CO., INC.
PITTSBURGH, PENNSYLVANIA 15222

All Rights Reserved
Copyright © 2002 by Christel Decker Bresko
No part of this book may be reproduced or transmitted
in any form or by any means, electronic or mechanical,
including photocopying, recording, or by any information
storage and retrieval system without permission in
writing from the publisher.

ISBN # 0-8059-5959-9
Printed in the United States of America

First Printing

For information or to order additional books, please write:
Dorrance Publishing Co., Inc.
643 Smithfield Street
Pittsburgh, Pennsylvania 15222
USA.
1-800-788-7654
Or visit our web site and on-line catalog at *www.dorrancepublishing.com*

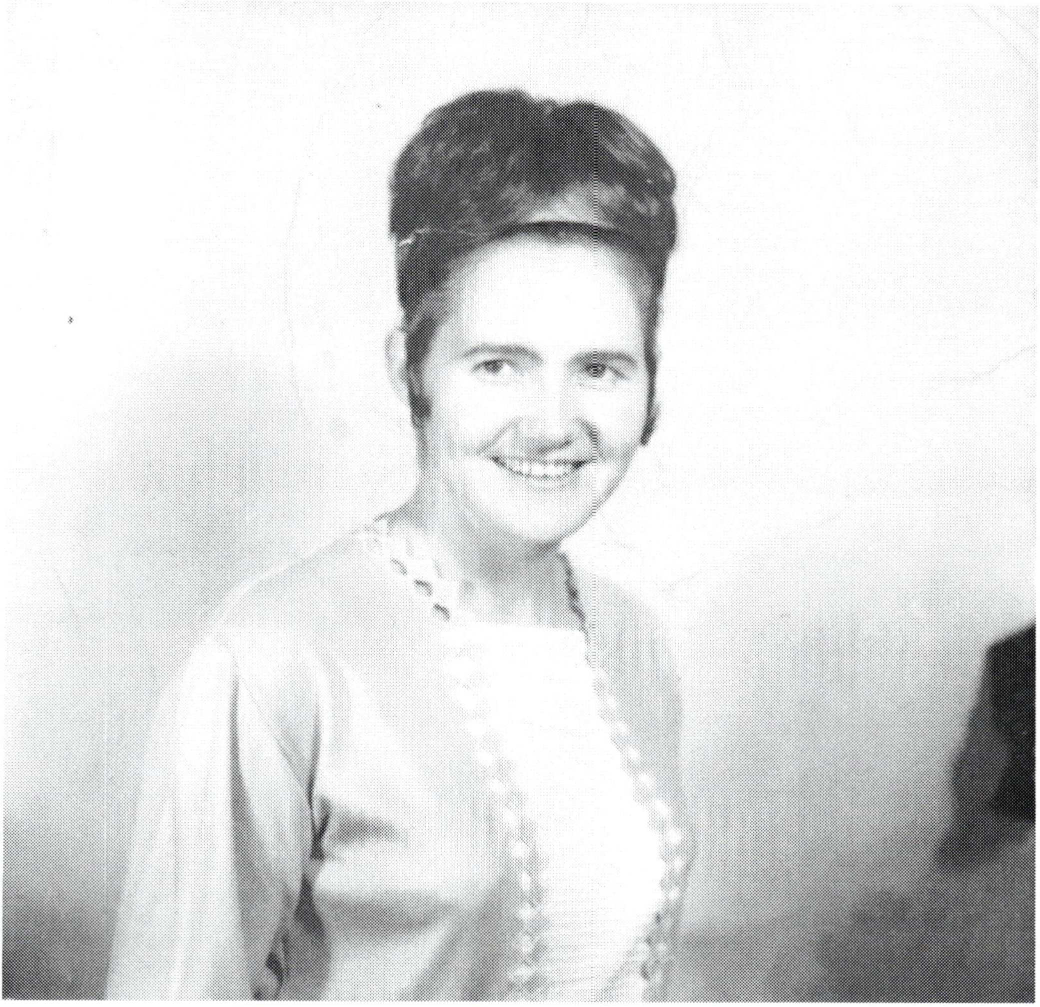

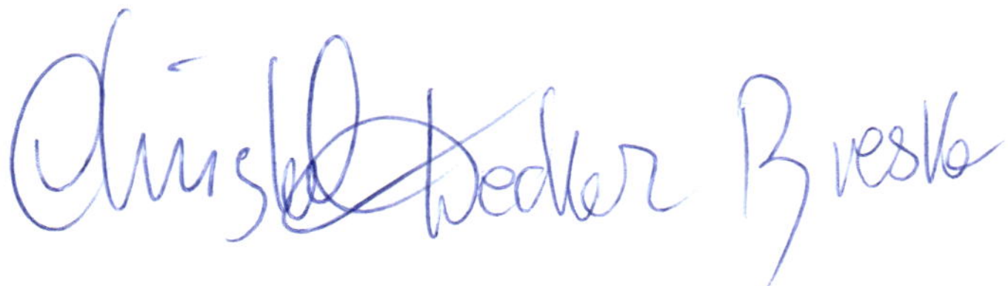

To God be the glory!

To all my family in Germany; to my husband, Bill, who was a great encouragement; Conny Schroder and Chris Stewart, who helped me along and assisted me greatly; and to all others who helped along the way.

Contents

My Parents	1
August 18, 1937	4
Wartime	6
My Mother and Me	8
My Little Brother	9
My Sister Was Lost	10
Childhood Diseases	12
My Brother Guenter	13
My Grown-up Little Brother	15
Childhood Sicknesses	17
Vaccinations for All the People	18
Childhood Mishaps	19
The Auction	21
Mom—Nurse to All	22
Aunt Dora	23
Aunt Frieda	24
If in Heaven There Are No Apples...	25
Hungry	26
Salt of the Earth	28
The Cemetery	30
Birds and Bees	31
Who Will Be First?	32
Beetlebugs	33
The Ruby Red Pitcher	34
Burning House	35
Summer	38
Childhood Days	39
Scream Louder	40
Wash Days	41
The Town Blackboard	43
The Bracelet	44
May 1945	46
Winter Wonderland	49

Advent Time	51
Es Weihnachtet sehr (Christmas)	52
Oh, Christmas Tree	54
A Month of December Not to Be Forgotten	57
My Dad in Russia	58
The Telegram	60
Dad's Arrival	62
There's a Man in the House	63
Moving	64
A New House, Bigger and Better	65
The House on the Poststreet	66
Washing Machines	68
Teen Years	69
A New Job	70
Ella	71
England	75
Midterm Nursing Exam	80
Squashed	82
Nursing at Nighttime	83
Big Eddy	84
Emergency Room	87
All about Moms and Babies	88
Friendship	89
Men's Medical	90
Twenty-four Roses	92
England/Germany	94
Kranken-Schwester/Velbert	96
Beroa Bible School	97
Greener Pasture	99
Internship in Hamburg	100
Hamburg Church Privacy	101
Hamburg Church Activities	102
Sister Crousart	104
Thinking of Leaving	106
1967	107

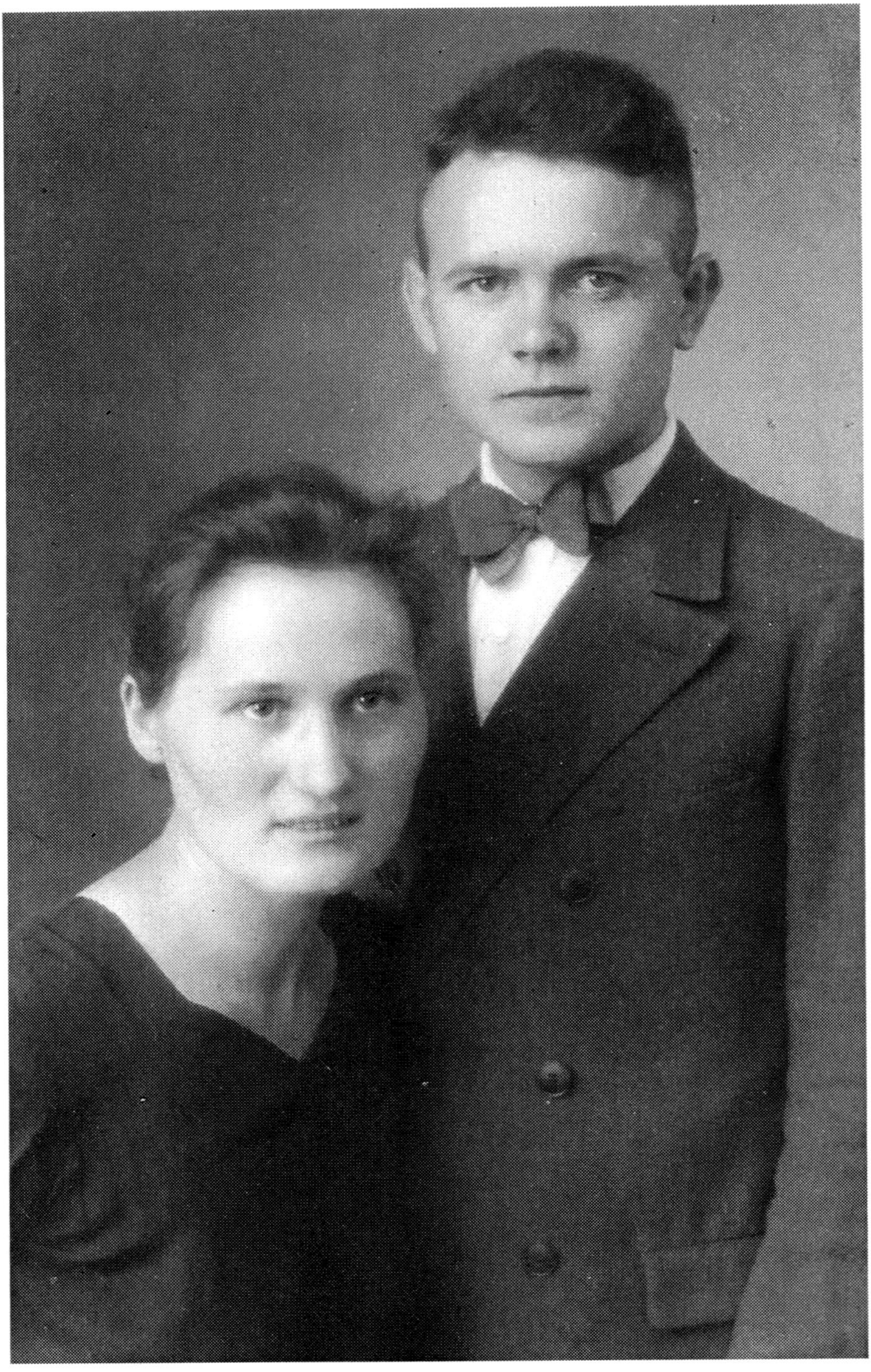

My Parents

Having godly parents is a great inheritance. I saw them pray and sing together, and hug each other.

Father had first joined the Nazi party when he was in his late teen years, however everybody his age had joined. So there was power in unity. "*Einheit macht stark*," was a quote Hitler used as a slogan.

Hitler had come to power and made great promises to the German people, but unemployment was at an all-time high. World War I was not quite forgotten yet, and Germany was still poverty-stricken. Mom recalled that during the inflation in 1929, to buy a loaf of bread one had to haul the money off in a wheelbarrow.

My most precious mother had a godly upbringing and was able to pray for things on earth and in heaven. She knew marriages were made in heaven and started to pray for her future husband, who at that time was following a regime not very godlike.

My dad knew my mom from his school years; she was just one year younger. Her friends and sisters did not think much of their friendship because he was a Nazi and a heathen, but Mom saw Dad as a very attractive, likeable, and handsome young man.

My grandmother, Mom's mother, was very sick and on her deathbed. Mom asked her just before she died what she thought about Oskar Decker, and she just said, "Go and get him!" Grandma gave her blessings and Mom ran with it.

They were married in December 1935. A lot of snow had fallen that night, and it seemed the earth had given its blessings and had made everything pure and holy. My father dressed in his uniform and Mother in pure white, and they were honored with the military guard, who had several flags raised on both sides, not in church but in the churchyard.

My dad became a Christian, and he knew he had to get away from the Nazi party. He had to make a move and resign, which was almost an impossible task without the help of God. He was threatened with courtmartial after the war was over, but God was in control and his name was erased, which became a great blessing in later years.

As a military man he served five years in the German army, then in 1945 he was taken as prisoner by the Russians and transported deep into Siberia until the year 1951.

Mother's future mother-in-law did not think much of her domestic skills, so on one occasion Oma (Grandma) handed mother some material for an apron to sew, but Mom tricked Oma by taking the material to her sister Martha and asked her to sew the apron while in return she would do her laundry, and it worked.

Opa (Grandpa) Henry thought a lot about Mom's work on the farm. He noticed that Minna's, my Mom's, work in the field was fast and efficient. Oma, however, still thought of her as only being able to open and close dainty curtains in the house, but Mom proved differently.

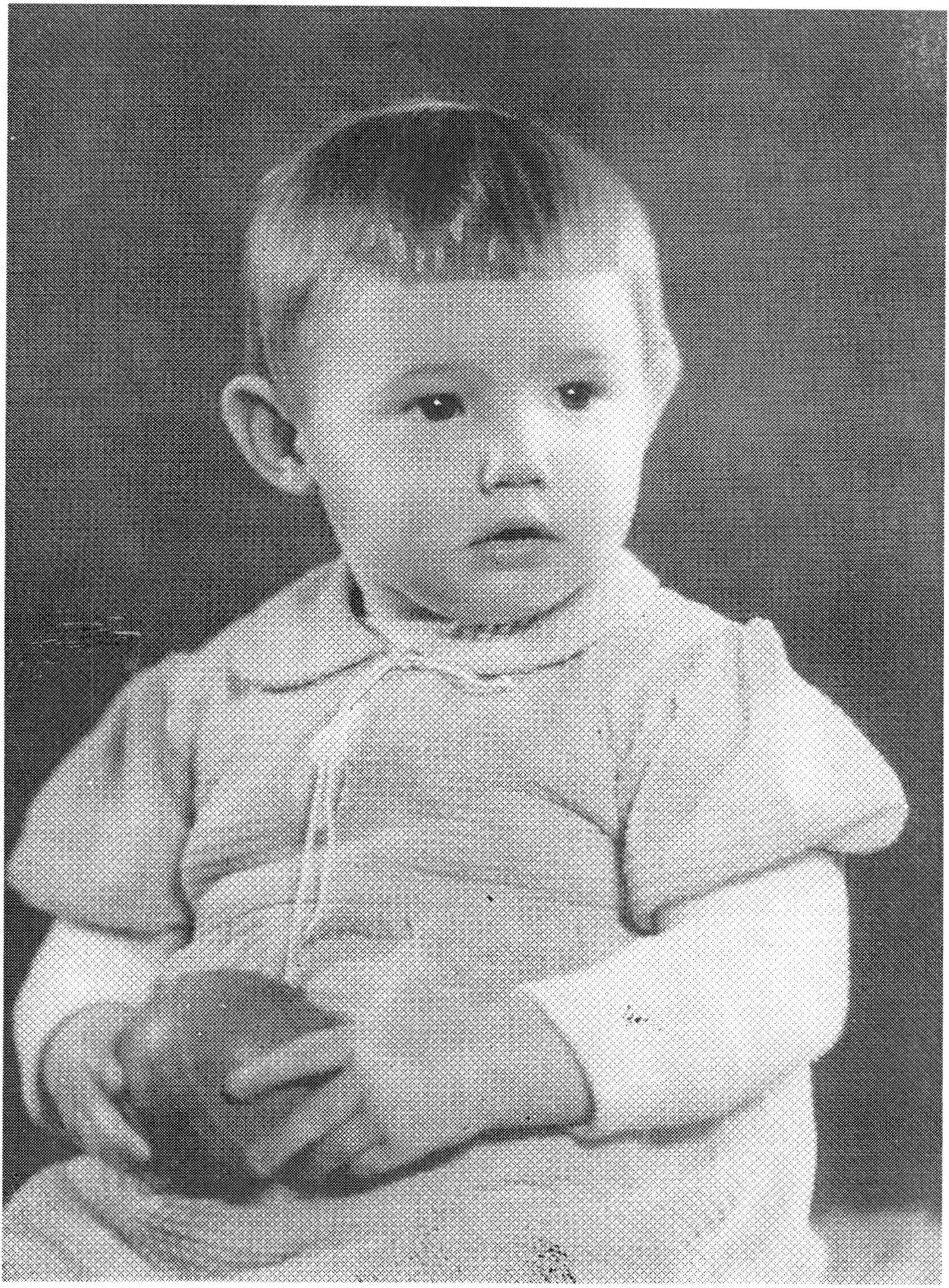

August, 18, 1937

It was a hot day when I was born. The midwife was called Wednesday and told Mom it would be a long labor. Aunt Maria was very eager to assist Mom, who was not pleased, so she told her sister the baby wouldn't be born just yet. Mom and Dad went for a walk just to let her know there was still time, so Aunt Maria went home. However Mom had to turn around quickly because the baby was coming! Aunt Maria had missed it all, but she became my godmother.

My sister, Inge, was born the following year in September and my brother, Guenter, two years later in October.

World War II was written in the wind; signs and rumors of war were in people's minds. My father was also registered and soon to be drafted. He left his small family January 1, 1940. Boot camp and training were his next assignments. As a little girl, I remember Dad in his uniform. He looked so attractive. His black leather boots were so shiny and clean. I also can remember the goodbyes and when Mom escorted him to the train station. We received letters that father was going to move far away from us to Norway. His expertise was in communication, especially Morse code.

Mom was all alone, taking care of us. We heard her pray, cry, and sing, and she taught stories from the Bible. Oh, I remember it so well, bedtime stories and sing alongs with the organ and guitar.

Father spent most of his war years in Norway. There was always great joy when a letter arrived or a package. Some of those letters were very special and Mother put them away in her nightstand. One day, my brother Guenter and a neighbor kid decided to play letter carrier and took all the letters and delivered them from door to door. He could not yet read himself, but he had a lot of joy delivering them. Of course Mom was very embarrassed that her love letters were enjoyed by the whole neighborhood.

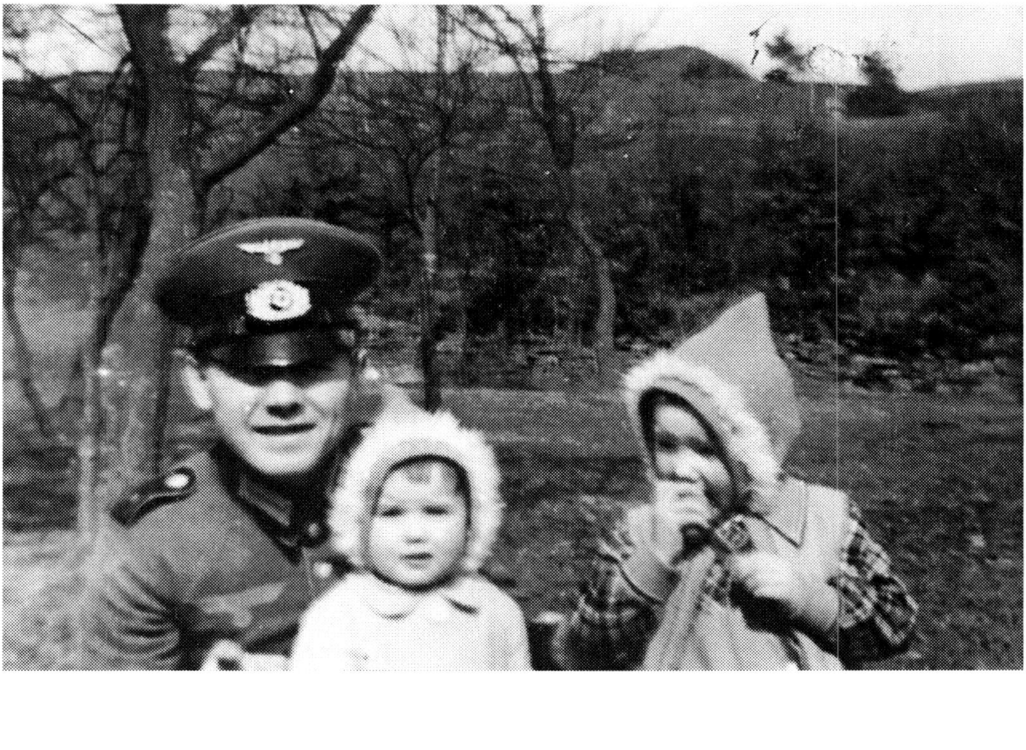

Wartime

War planes flying overhead, bombs falling, people being shot at—it was wartime.

The sirens went off day and night. One moment we were in school, the next moment in a bunker or basement. Dinners were interrupted and sleepless nights were common to us because of the howling of planes when they passed over the town. The low-flying airplanes shot everything that was moving.

A trainful of refugees from Hungary arrived and parked in our town at the railroad station. Many of the younger population was fascinated by all the tanks and guns. They let us go inside and play, searching out those big cannonballs while pretending to shoot the enemy.

My sister, my brother, and I were some of those investigators. However, when the siren blasted off and everyone looked for cover, all the Hungarians grabbed their children and belongings—grabbing us as well—then ran for cover in the forest nearby. Mom knew we were playing and frantically she looked for us in the railway station, but no one was there. Then she headed for the forest, where she found us children face down on the ground, taking cover from those low-flying airplanes. My sister and I had my brother, who was only five years old at the time, between us. There were quiet times as well, but we never knew when the next siren would blast off.

It was the evening of March 30, 1944, when a bomber from England was shot down. The bomber was on the way to Nuremberg for a large bombing raid and had just missed our town. It flew almost over our house, across the river Aar (our most famous swimming spot), then crashed into the Hain forest. We saw everything from our kitchen window—a mighty bang, then more flames.

People came running from everywhere but no one could get close because of all the explosions going off. It was a fifteen-minute walk from our place to the crash site. Different stories were told from those who saw the crash and heard it. Someone had seen a man who had ejected hanging in a tree. Several people were dead, but one alive, although pinned under some metal.

The plane had split into half and large pieces were scattered all over the forest. It seemed from our window that all the trees were in flames.

The story was told that a plane heading for Nuremberg in south Germany was hit and was going down in the foothills of the Westerwald in Herbornseelbach, County Hessen.

Mom would wake me up to listen to the airplanes flying over our place. At times a cluster of planes heading for bigger cities were right over us. They sounded so eerie. I still can hear them when I think about it. I remember the whole sky lit up like a Christmas tree. Mom would say, "They are staking out a town, then the enemies are going to bomb it." From our bedroom window we looked south and saw Frankfurt and Giesen in flames.

A nurse friend of Mom's who was taking care of mentally ill patients came late one night to just talk and ask for advice. She had been assigned to go on a train trip with about fifty patients to take them to a concentration camp at Dachau.

There were a lot of secrets around the town and no one wanted to talk because it was very dangerous to help Jews or people on the hit lists. Mom only told her to get out of it and not go on that train ride.

Mom had worked for Jewish people in her younger years and held them in very high esteem. She had talked so highly of them that I wanted to see a Jewish person. I was sure they all had haloes around their heads.

We had some Jewish friends living in our hometown, but they were taken away overnight and never heard from again. Mom told us later they were picked up by the Gestapo and sent away.

My Mother and Me

The war was in full swing. Bombs were flying all around us, and low-flying airplanes were shooting anything moving. So we were all taught to lie down or look for a bunker when we heard the first sound of planes. The sirens had different functions—short or long and howling up or down. We children knew what to do next—either run home, lay flat, or hide. There was no time to get scared. Only the adults were afraid because they knew more than us children. We had wooden guns to play with, so we stood in the yard and tried to shoot those enemy planes down.

I became a sleepwalker, so I needed to be watched at night. Once Mother had found me sitting on a still quite warm stove. Another time she found me barefooted outside in the snow. It was always dark, and black covers were hung over the windows. We had no lights in the streets and very little light in the house, and I often took the covers down just to see a little daylight.

Mom had put me to bed with all the other children, but I started to wander off and sailed down a flight of stairs, ending up on a ceramic tile floor with only a bump on my head. However all the adults in the house thought a bomb had gone through the roof.

Prisoners from Poland had occupied and settled in our school. They came around trading hand-carved toys for some bread or milk. The German people also had appliances fixed.

We had a prisoner come to our home, and Mom asked if he could fix her aluminum washbowl. He took it and had it soldered and returned it. I also knew our night potty had a hole in it. We had not used it for a while since Mom had sent us to the outside toilet. That meant going down the stairs, out of the house, and around the yard to the only toilet we had for two families, which was next to the stable, hoping no one would be on it. Again there was never any light.

Mom was embarrassed when I showed up with the potty, but he only motioned that it was very much okay and indicated with his hands that he also had little children. It was not very long before we had our potty fixed.

My Little Brother

Guenter wanted to be a real working man, taking the place of my dad, who was in the war, but it was one of those rain-drenched days when he wanted to go outside and play. A five-year-old little boy could easily fall down into a storm drain and be washed away, and we had no paved roads. All our walkways were very muddy and slick, so there was plenty of dirt to be found.

At suppertime, Mom called and looked for him. She saw one little boy but did not think much of it and kept on calling. That little boy stood right in front of her and Mother could not recognize him, he was so dirty and full of mud. His hands and face had taken on a totally different color. Guenter looked at Mother and said, "Mom, I am a working man!"

That same little boy had dressed himself one morning very quietly in two pairs of pants and a shirt over a pullover. "Mom," he said, "I want to run away." She replied, "Where do you want to go to?"

"Momma, I don't know but I am leaving."

"Well, we are going to miss you," she said, trying to cry. She packed him a little lunch, put it in a little bag, and hung it on a stick for him to carry on his back. Mom also placed a few coins in his pocket, then Guenter said goodbye to all of us and went out of the house and down the street.

Mother kept a close eye on him, though. She watched him walking along the road, then he came to a stop, turned around, and came back. Mother welcomed him and said, "Oh, you are back so soon already!" Guenter, with tears in his eyes, said, "Oh, Momma, I was so homesick for you!"

My Sister was Lost

My sister was lost. She was seven years old at the time and sirens were going off, which meant full alarm and all people had to seek shelter, but my sister was nowhere to be found. Mother ran up and down the streets calling her name. The police grabbed Mom and pulled her into a nearby bunker. Frantically she escaped the very crowded hideout and again started searching for my sister.

It was later when people started looking in the neighborhood. On our side of the street were old dugouts (foxholes) left by the soldiers with a foot of water in them. When my sister had heard the siren, dutifully she had looked for somewhere to hide and crawled into one of those holes.

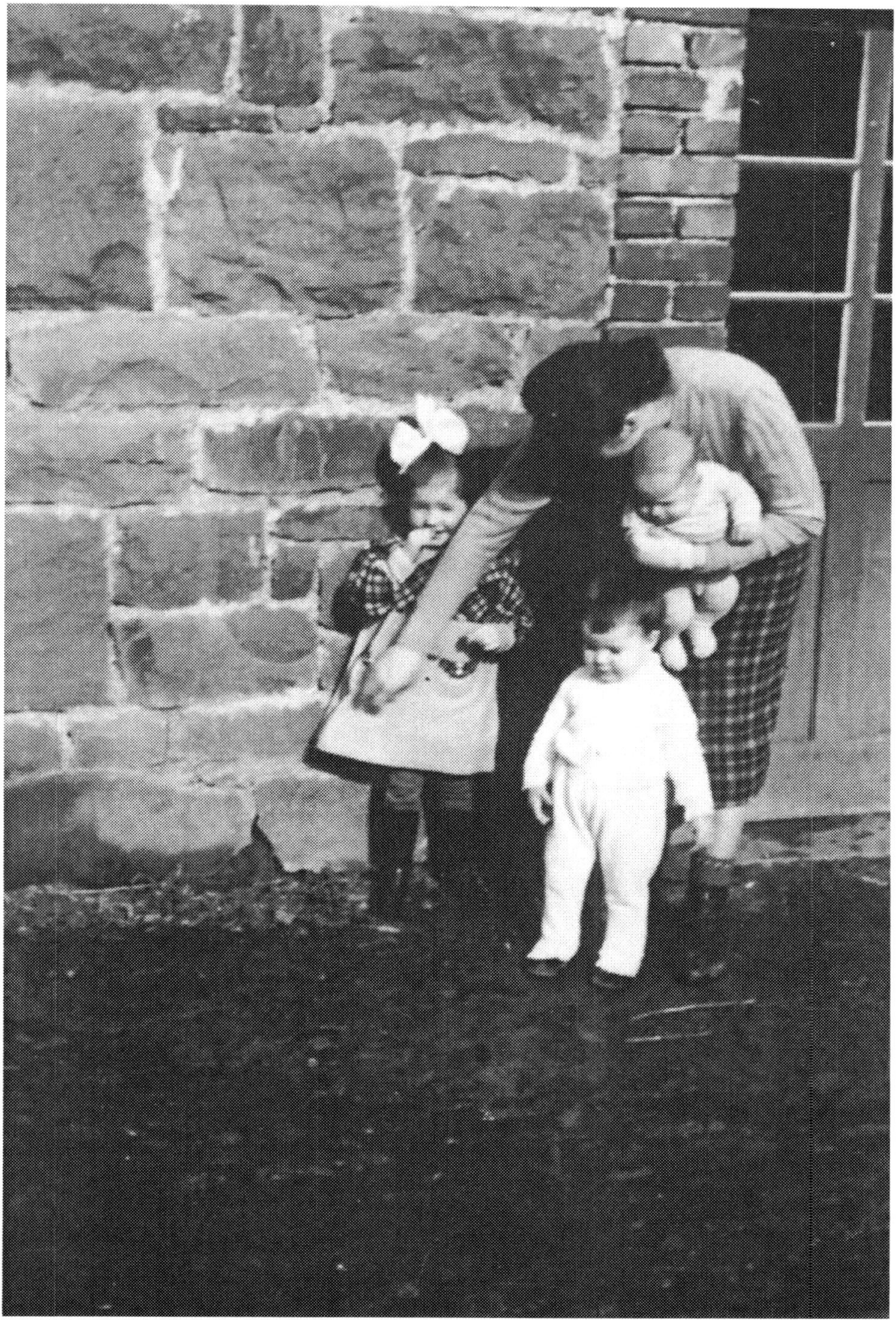

Childhood Diseases

My sister, Inge, developed meningitis at the age of three years along with double pneumonia.

My dad was already serving in the war in Norway as a radio communicator, so my mom requested furlough but was refused by the commanding officer in charge. Only when the request came from the town mayor was a special home tour granted for my father.

The doctors had told my mother there was no hope for my sister and she might have permanent brain damage, a diagnosis my dear godly mother would not accept.

Mom had to sign plenty of release papers allowing her to take full responsibility to keep my sister at home. The other option was to put my sister into one of those clinics where the Nazi doctors would do experiments on her brain. However my cousin had just died at the hands of these Nazi doctors, and my mother was not about to send her to those hospitals.

After eight weeks of Inge's illness, my father came home. My sister had not even sat up in bed once, had only drank water, and had chewed the crusts of rye bread my mother had peeled off. She was too weak to cry and only whimpered.

Mom had been by my sister's bedside for many weeks, day and night. When my father finally arrived, he entered the bedroom, took my sister from the crib, sat her on his knees, and said, "Inge, come and let's eat."

From then on, new life entered my sister's body. Her strength was renewed day by day, and with much prayer and our dad's presence, she became healthy, strong, and was perfectly normal.

In later years, Inge attended the school of higher learning, but married quite early and raised four fine children, all serving the Lord in several capacities and in various churches in Germany. The power of prayer was quite evident in our household.

My Brother Guenter

While in fourth grade, Guenter started to complain about his right leg. He eventually walked with a limp, but the doctors could not find anything wrong. Mom started to get worried. She changed doctors and was told after some intensive tests that he had tuberculosis in his right hip joint. Soon after my brother was put in a cast from his waist down. The right leg was in a cast down to his toes and the left leg down to the knee. His legs were spread apart, and a handle was put between his legs for transportation.

All this had changed our family. Guenter needed around-the-clock care only my mother could give, so we adapted as much as we could and life went on. My sister and I helped as much as we could. We had placed Guenter in an old baby carriage and took him to school as often as possible, since school was not very far—just down the road, well within walking distance. Mom had a special seat made for him on the bicycle so he did not miss out on picnics or other outings.

Uncle Karl, our landlord, made my brother a special outside bed with a canopy over it so he was able to get plenty of fresh air and saw people passing by in rain, sunshine, or snow.

His eating habits were not much to talk about, although Mom received extra money to buy butter and milk and was concerned about his weight. Food was not very plentiful since we still had to deal with rations. Mom did not let us feed Guenter because Inge and I would just stick a finger in his food, and he was done eating.

Every so often, Guenter was placed in the hospital for x-rays and a change of the cast. Sometimes he stayed about two weeks at a time, so Mom would visit him three times a week from 2:00 to 4:00 P.M. and on Sundays whenever the doors were open. We children could not go because we were not old enough. Money was scarce, so Mother walked because there was no money for the train or bus. Then an older woman who was visiting someone else in the hospital gave Mom money for the train and told her she did not want to see her walking anymore. So Mom went to the train station and pretended to buy a ticket, but turned around and walked again and bought food with the money. In her mind, a train ticket was a lot of money to spend on such a luxury as traveling by train. Mother was always very thin because all the excess food she gave to us children.

After one year and three months, the cast had come off for good.

The cast was off now and physiotherapy was planned for the next few weeks. It was a most painful ordeal. Mom knew more about it since she heard Guenter yell and scream when the therapists tried to bend his legs and make him walk.

He had lost a lot of weight. When he finally came home to stay, neighbors, friends, and family brought extra food and soon he became more round.

A neighbor came around and demonstrated his new bike, and Guenter just wanted to stand on the one pedal while the neighbor boy guided it down the road. Guenter's leg was not strong enough to carry his weight. He slipped and fell on the road, yelling, "Mom, my leg is broken!" Yes, the x-rays showed he had a break just below his right knee. Guenter was again placed in a leg cast for six weeks.

Mom was well known in the hospital when she arrived with my brother. A doctor sang a soldier's song for her: "*Tapfere kleine Soldaten Frau*" ("You brave little soldier's wife"). Mom made room for her tears.

My Grown-up Little Brother

Guenter was granted another six-week vacation to recuperate after his fall from the bike. The welfare system of Germany had resorts near the ocean or in the mountains, as well as on farms, for youngsters with tuberculosis.

Mom had to pack a suitcase for him and take him to a nearby town, where he was going to be picked up with other young boys by trained personnel.

There was absolutely no visitation, so our young brother was on his own for a long time. He did write and ask for money, his explanation was he did not think Mother wanted him to starve.

His return day was planned and Mother was to pick him up. It was a very hot August day. Guenter arrived with other young boys, and Mom could not believe her eyes. Oh my, did he ever gain weight! He hardly could move. He had his coat on, so she asked him to take it off because it was so very hot, and in a very determined voice he said, "No, Mother!" So Mom had to try something else and said, "Let's go to the bathroom!" They went and she was soon aware of Guenter's predicament. He wore two pairs of pants and under that a pair of long johns and all his underwear, as well as two shirts and a sweater. "Guenter, how come you are wearing everything on top of each other?"

"Well, Mother, I was unable to close my suitcase, so what I could not get into the suitcase I put on."

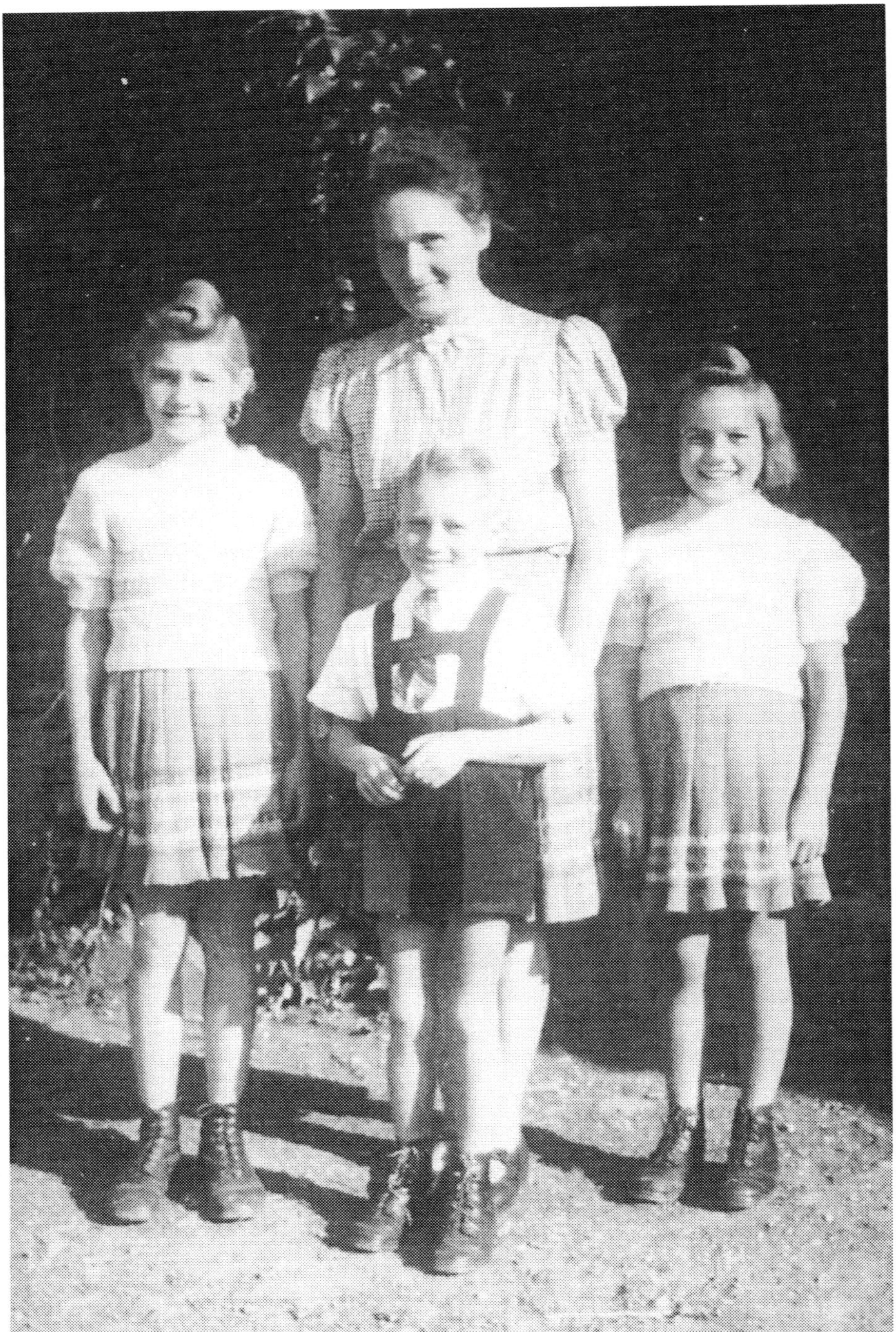

Childhood Sicknesses

My school day was over and I felt very sick, sore all over, and had a swollen neck. My throat looked very red and I could hardly even swallow water.

Mom had informed the town nurse and was told that measles was getting the best of the children. Therefore, when I became red and hot all over my body, I was diagnosed with having measles. Mother did not wait for the rest of the family to come home and complain. She put us all to bed together and waited for the outcome, so we children were all sick together and getting well together.

Diphtheria had also showed its ugly face. One of our school friends had died in a nearby hospital and Gretel, the daughter of our landlord, was told to go to the funeral. However, she did not want to go for fear she also would get that disease. But her mother told her it would not be possible to get infected because she did not die at home.

Gretel obeyed her parents and went, but in her own words she told us she stayed away from the funeral procession and did not go near the grave. She said she saw all those bacteria heading straight toward her. Two days later, she had diphtheria and our whole household was quarantined for six weeks.

We were still at war and she had a special place in the basement, all wrapped up in blankets and away from us children. Her mother was the only one who could go near her, wearing medical gown and mask.

However the diphtheria sign came in very handy later.

X-rays were taken at school and Mom was told I had something suspicious on my lungs and needed medical attention. I was diagnosed with tuberculosis when I was twelve years old, so Mother had a choice of leaving me at home to stay in bed all day or taking me to a sanatorium where children were hospitalized with that disease. She decided on the latter because it would be very hard on the whole family to keep me in bed all day, not feeling too sick. I had been running a low fever for quite a while, and it had always been a puzzle of late. Eventually, I went for three months to that sanatorium and was sent home with a good report.

Vaccinations for All the People

There was a notice that everyone in town needed to be vaccinated for everything that could ail a person from diphtheria to small pox to polio. Needles! My sister was so deathly afraid of them that when she needed a haircut and she saw a white coverall, she became frantic so Mom asked the barber if he could take his barbering overcoat off for a while.

When my sister was so sick with pneumonia and meningitis some years ago, needles were daily occurrences, and somehow she had not forgotten it.

Mom stood in line with us three children to get vaccinated. She looked around, unable to locate my sister, and then had to get out of that long line with my brother and me and hunt for my sister. Now she had to start all over again, standing in line to be vaccinated.

Because there was tuberculosis in our family, we had received a notice from our family doctor to get a blood test, so Mother had gotten us ready. We were supposed to not eat that morning and had to walk two hours (which was a shortcut). When we arrived and the doctor greeted us, he asked if we had been fasting. We answered, "Oh, we brushed our teeth and some water did go down into our stomach," hoping this would mean no blood test. But the doctor did it anyway, and my sister passed out and fell on the floor!

Childhood Mishaps

I was the oldest of us three children, so mother depended on me to do more grown-up chores like hauling, carrying, and fetching things.

The stairs leading to our apartment were very steep and slick from waxing, which was to prevent the wood from deteriorating and rotting. Mom kept those stairs very shiny. There were about twenty steps with quite a turn halfway up.

We walked those steps many times daily, but one Sunday Mom trusted me with a glass bowl to deliver to the landlady downstairs. I was in first grade and very proud when Mom gave me an important chore. Something distracted me from the window and I was not looking where I was going, so I sailed down the flight of stairs with the bowl in my hands. I finally landed on the bottom ceramic tile floor.

Blood was gushing and pulsating from my hand. Mom came running and Aunt Luise, the landlady, who was milking, heard my fall and also came running with a large towel. She wrapped the towel around my small, almost severed hand, which was barely hanging on by some skin. Blood was seeping through the towel and I went into shock. It was not long before I was unconscious. I was told at a later date that I had lost a lot of blood and had vomited all over the car.

When I awoke from surgery, I was in my own bed with a large cast on my right hand. I had become very weak and needed to stay in bed for a few days.

The time had come for me to have my cast changed in the same hospital where I was stitched up a week ago. There was no money for train fares so Mom and I walked. Mom knew a shortcut, but it was still a long way through the hills and valley and crossing a creek—about a two-hour walk one way.

The next few weeks Mom and I walked that road three times a week. Then my hand got severely infected and we had to make a special trip to the doctor. Pus was coming through my bandage, a blister had formed on top of my hand, and I itched severely.

The nurse and doctor yelled at me to keep my hand still. My hand was held over a container while the doctor cut away my bandage and removed the stitches. Mom tried her best to keep me calm but noticed nervousness settling into her system.

I never did receive any pain pills or something to calm me down, and Mom was crying on the way out and I was very unhappy. If having difficulties at the hospital was not enough, there was always a big dog, a German shepherd that came running from someone's yard, ready to take us on every time we walked by a certain house at the edge of the forest.

Even on the weekend we thought about our upcoming trip to the hospital on Monday and dodging that big dog. On Monday morning, though, Mom and I got on our knees, praying to God of the universe for special guidance and protection and calmness at the hospital. When we reached the edge of the forest looking for the dog, there was no more dog and we never saw it again.

Mom and I entered the hospital. When we were called into the doctor's office, to our surprise he welcomed us to sit down and said, "Frau Decker, you were in my dreams last night." Mother, not knowing what to say, only looked and him and said, "Oh, well." Our visits were much more pleasant from then on. I even received candies.

The Auction

Fall was just around the corner, and the community trees with all kinds of fruits were going to be auctioned off. Mom and we three children were eager to go and try our luck. There were hundreds of people, all trying their luck as well. Many trees were on the auction block since plums and apples were plentiful that year.

The crew was moving really fast, and Mom had gone ahead to look for a tree to her liking. She saw one tree with red apples, and when the auctioneer started the bidding, Mom raised her hand and started the bid with five DM (five dollars). There was total silence—no one said anything. No one raised a hand. The auctioneer looked around the place, but it seemed we were it. The bid was closed and we had over one hundred pounds of apples. Mom told us later that the Almighty God had kept the lion's mouth shut so many years ago, and he had done it again.

We were very desperate for some food. All our rations were gone, the shelves were empty, and there was no money. The only way out was to pray, and that we did. That evening we found an envelope with twenty DM shoved under our front door.

Mom—Nurse to All

Aunt Elisabeth, Mom's sister, needed help. She was in one of those teaching hospitals in Marburg/Lahn run by the Hitler regime. Her husband, who was also in the war, was unable to assist her.

It was early in the morning when Mom received a note from someone unknown to her, written (or rather, scribbled) by her sister, Elisabeth, to come as soon as possible and take her home. She had been scheduled for brain surgery that day.

In those days, car or taxi transportation was very rare, so with much waiting and praying, Mom located a driver with a car. It was an hour drive through the back country. Mom was very much in thought, hoping not to miss getting there before it was too late. It was very difficult to locate my aunt in that large hospital, but Mom finally found her on the fifth floor.

Her room was full of doctors and nurses who were very surprised to see a visitor. Mother bent over Aunt Elisabeth, kissed her, and asked in a low voice, "Do you still want to go home?" With a grunt she said, "Take me home." This was enough for Mother, who started dressing Aunt Elisabeth while everyone watched and wondered about the turn of events.

Someone handed Mother a stack of papers to sign and she signed them all, not quite knowing the content of the paperwork. Suddenly she found herself alone in the room with Aunt Elisabeth. Just getting away from the hospital was in both of their minds.

However Aunt Elisabeth could not stand or walk. There was neither an elevator nor wheelchair, so Mother carried Aunt Elisabeth from the fifth floor all the way down to the car.

For many weeks to come, Mom cared for her sister all alone until strength came back into her bones. Aunt Elisabeth's daughter, Helen, also lived with us during this time.

Aunt Dora

We did not know Aunt Dora too well. She was the wife of one of my father's brothers.

Once mother received money from Aunt Dora to come up and visit her. At that time traveling was very difficult, but Mother told us three children that we were going on a journey by train.

The trip was a three-hour train ride with many passengers on board. Although it was difficult to get a seat, Mom made sure none of us children had to stand, or at least not stand for very long.

When a need arose and someone needed a seat, Mom would say, "If one of my children gives you a seat, you will allow them to sit on your lap." Since we were children, we did not have enough strength to stand for very long, so Mother made sure we had a seat.

For the last portion of the journey we had to change to a bus. There was hardly any room to stand, let alone to sit. Inge, my sister, did not feel good, so someone gave her a peppermint candy, which fell on the floor. Inge tried to find it, and when she saw it, she put her foot on it to save it. A lady gave her another peppermint, but on the way out of the bus, Inge crawled on the floor between the legs of the people, trying to find that precious piece of candy.

Mother had some marriage counseling to do so we children played outside, going places with Ottie and Rudy, the two older children. Kassel was a big city. I cannot recall buying anything, but I had my very first ice cream there in one of the ice cream parlors. It was a very pretty bowl, with white ice cream and a red line across. Oh, did we children savor it; it had a lasting effect on us.

Aunt Frieda

Aunt Frieda, a second cousin of my mother, had been confined to a wheelchair for many years. She never complained. Aunt Frieda always sat on a hard chair in front of the table, looking out the window. Her husband got her out of bed before he went to work, then relatives like my mom and Aunt Elisabeth took turns checking on her.

As small children, we knew the way to Aunt Frieda's house. Mother would tell us to go to her house after kindergarten.

One day when I was about five years old and my sister was four, we arrived at her home but found her still in bed, all alone. When she saw the two of us, she started to cry. My sister and I helped her to get on the commode and then on her chair. I remember climbing up on her bed to turn her around while my sister held on to her legs. Somehow we managed to help swing her, holding onto her while pivoting her on the chair.

Mother told us later Aunt Frieda had prayed for someone to come and heard the Lord say two angels were on the way.

If in Heaven There Are No Apples…

As a child, I enjoyed all kinds of fruit, but mostly apples. After the war, when I first ate a banana, I told my mother I could remember the taste but was sure I had never eaten a banana, but my mother told me my dad fed me bananas at an early age. I longed for strawberries, raspberries, and plums, but apples were highest on my list. So one day I informed my mother that if in heaven there are no apples, I did not wish to go there!

Mother was unable to buy apples and we did not own an apple tree, so mother took a train ride to the Rhine valley where apples were available for trade or by just picking up the fallen apples from the ground. Taking a train was very risky, because they were shot at, but trains remained the only transportation for the German people. The trains were full to capacity, with people on the train roof and hanging onto guardrails between the train cars.

Mother once found a place on the outside steps leading into the train. When she came home, we saw her scraped knees from when the train passed through a tunnel or came close to a wall—all because of some apples. Mom brought home two suitcases full and handed me the biggest apple, commenting it was almost as big as my head. Other people craved chocolate, but I wanted an apple.

In later years when food was more plentiful, Mom once counted twenty apple cores left by my sister and me on our nightstand. When Inge married, she and her husband and three children had all different kinds of fruit trees, as well as vegetables and chickens. Their home also had a large garden, so it was a self-contained little gentleman farm, as I recall it. Inge was very fortunate to live near a farmer's market, a bakery, and a grocery store, which were all within walking distance.

Hungry

Many times we went to bed hungry.

Mother went shopping; it seemed, always on credit. When the war started, her oil pot was empty and, as she told us, she never could catch up, so she went shopping and then paid for the last month's groceries.

Aunt Martha had a store, so Mom felt free to buy and pay later. Sometimes we were sent to the baker to buy extra bread and to pay later, but we often told Mother, "If we don't have the money, we won't eat." Mother made sure we always had enough potatoes for the winter, so potatoes were in our daily diet. She knew many ways to cook potatoes, but fat was missing, so we ate boiled potatoes and pancakes. However I liked the potato dumplings.

We collected beech nuts in the woods, then Mother would save them to have them pressed for oil. Once she came home from grocery shopping and had one hundred grams (about two to three ounces) of bacon. Oh, we all knew about it! She wanted it just for flavoring, but where was it? It was missing.

After a very intense search, we found my sister under the table, devouring our monthly supply of bacon. There was great sorrow in our home. We seemed to be so hungry for anything with fat.

We did not have meat, nor did we have sausage, because Mother traded the meat stamps for the more necessary items such as bread and milk. But once a year, on our birthday, we received a ring of bologna with a red ribbon around it. Mother divided the meat sausage, with the biggest part given to the one who had a birthday.

There was no compassion from the government. Every Sunday during wartime an official came by to collect money for the German army. They would ask her how much the Sunday meal would cost, and then he collected the amount and told us to make soup. It was called "Sunday soup money." There was never enough money to go around, so they did not get much from us.

Mother saw to it that we always had some kind of food and more than she did. She would say, "I will just adjust my belt around the waist."

"Give us this day our daily bread"—Oh, how Mother would rely on that verse! There were blessings, such as people would send food. For instance, when they slaughtered a pig (usually in November when it was starting to get cold), we would get invited for a meal. We children often commented that their food tasted better than Mother's, who often cooked without any fat. She would say, "Children, give me a piece of meat and I can cook."

It was the time when my brother received extra rations because of his illness, so Mom had a little extra butter in the house. It was then that my brother asked, "Momma, may I have a cut on the side of my bread?" Well, we were wondering—why a cut? So he explained, "When Momma spreads the butter on the bread, there is always a little extra butter on the knife, and instead of putting it back in the butter dish, with a cut on the side of the bread I can have a little extra butter."

One of the neighbor ladies (they were farmers) asked Mother if she would sew a dress for her little girl for Easter. Mom said, "Yes, in exchange for a roast." The lady laughed and said, "Oh my, Minna, you are a big joker." Well, Mother sewed the dress but never received anything for it.

During the school year, we were also always hungry. For breakfast Mom would ask each of us, "How would you like to have your bread this morning, wet or dry, with sugar or salt?"

At times we were all so hungry, Mom just said, "Let's go for a walk." So we went to the hills, barely able to climb. Then we laid and looked at the sky with all the cloud formations and seemed to forget our hunger for a moment.

Our garden was a place of refuge and the brook brought much enjoyment. Mother heard the brook talk and repeated its "water talk" to us children. We also played and made dams or a waterfall.

In the fall, Mom dug up the whole garden by hand with a spade, for the winter. We were surrounded by farmers, so she did what she could to not appear lazy. The farmers seemed to have food, but she worked all day for one farmer and came home with only one cucumber for pay, although she never complained.

Salt of the Earth

Mother did a lot of visitations in town. She knew many people—older people, sick people, and struggling young couples, and at times we would go along. Mother would hold a hand, pray, do dishes, or clean floors—whatever was needed. She would always take flowers from her garden. Dahlias were her favorite, which grew so tall we children could play hide and seek among the stems.

Once Father had sent a package with real coffee beans in a coffee can, so Mother counted out beans and distributed them to people who really needed a good cup of coffee.

During the war, there was no salt in the stores. On day Mom was told a freight train was stranded somewhere along the railroad tracks, a half-day's journey away. Each carrying a bag, Mom, my sister, and I and people from the neighborhood walked all the way to the stranded train. We stayed close to the forest so as not to be noticed from the air. The warplanes were still very active and were shooting at anything that moved. We made that long journey to and from without any difficulties. There was a lot of salt for us to load up and carry home.

Mom and other people would drink artificial coffee by putting wheat or rye or any grain, on top of the stove or oven and roast it to get the right brown color, then brew it in boiling water to make a drink from it. We called it "cowboy coffee."

In the back of the stove, a small cooking pot with sour milk would cook and simmer to make "cook cheese" so milk would never go to waste. We usually had sour milk after a thunderstorm and were told many bacteria would saturate the air and milk would curdle. This special homemade cheese was a real treat after having salt or sugar on our sandwich. We had no refrigerator in those days, so food that spoiled was usually kept in the basement where it was cool. We had a butter crock in which water covered the butter, which kept it cool.

Mother was a very creative cook, but she had to keep it simple because we had no meat or sausages to enhance our meals.

Beans were a steady diet, and one time I rebelled about eating beans again. I became stubborn at the table, and Mother even more so. So at 3 P.M., I was still sitting with my bowl of beans, not at the table anymore but on the stairway to the attic. Mother was not about to give up, as I had found out. My thinking was to slowly open the window to the attic and throw my bowl and all those ugly looking beans out on the street. Mom had caught on and made sure my evil plan was not about to be carried out. My playing time was cut very short, so I finally gave in and never tried this scheme again.

Easter was not far off, and my grandma told my mom to send us three children to her farm to get some Easter eggs. My other cousins and their mother lived with Grandma, so they were always first to get the milk, eggs, and meat, and Grandma did not have much control over her household. On Easter Sunday, all three of us children, full of expectation, walked to Grandma's house with our Easter baskets, and Grandma had only one egg for us and my sister Inge carried it. I think Mother was more hurt than we children were. We never did go again and ask for anything. Mom would say, "Children, come—we do not need it."

Momma's favorite cheese recipe (or "Quick Cheese")
1 pound sour milk
1/2 teaspoon salt to taste
1 1/2 teaspoons baking soda
1 teaspoon caraway seeds

Mix well in a crock pot. Cover it and leave everything for about two to three hours in a warm place until glossy. Use it on an open-face sandwich, preferably German home-baked rye bread with fresh chives or marmalade.

Mom knew when the strawberries were ripe in the hills. These berries were so little, but made up for it in taste. It took us children all morning to fill our cup since we had eaten some, dropped some, and shared some with others. Mother had picked the most, and at home we had strawberry delight with just plain sugar and milk. Very few times did Mom have enough to make jam.

All the school children had to collect berries, everything that grew wild from rosehips to raspberries, blueberries, and wild currants. School time was used for that activity as a field trip ordered by the school district. Mom was very good and encouraged us to go and pick for the school and then for us. Come fall, there was hardly anything to pick where the school children had been. Everyone kept their little place secret. Nothing was wasted.

The Cemetery

Mother had me go to kindergarten at a very early age and a shortcut was over the wall and through the cemetery which was used by children from the neighborhood. It was a little difficult for the adults, but some did it as well. We knew exactly where to plant our feet, then swing our little bodies over the wall. Then we would do a big leap into the bushes, trying to miss the graves, which were quite old and some of them were caving in.

Often we played hide and seek or tag. The children from our side of town were usually in control. We knew the dark places in the cemetery and had a way not to be found for a long time.

I know now that Mother was not too fond of us playing on that so-called sacred plot. But since we were living just a few feet away from the cemetery, she did not want to put fear into our little lives. Mother told us that our dead neighbors were the most peaceful friends around which we told others.

It was very dark and late one night as Mother walked along the road beside the cemetery. As she came closer to our home she saw a flickering light and heard a steady knock against the stone wall. There was no other light, no street light. All the windows were blacked out because of the war. Mother was in a state of panic as she called out "Karl!" our landlord and uncle's name.

A light came from the corner where we usually climbed the wall. Mom ventured closer to our home, hoping this spookiness would pass and she would be saved from all evil. Well, it was Uncle Karl! He was cleaning his smoke pipe, banging it against the wall to clean it out.

Birds and Bees

We children had decided we needed another baby, and Mom agreed. It was 1942 and Dad was still in Norway as a soldier. So on our own we did some investigating.

We were told we had to put candies or sugar on the windowsill, so we chose four windows—three for us, and one for Mom to keep track of.

In kindergarten we were told to check in a cistern with a heavy iron lid near a hill. We had invited other children who told us about it to come with us, and when we put our ears close to the lid, we could all hear the babies cry! There also was a lot of water in the cistern making splashes, but we could hear babies cry and wondered how we could get to them.

Daily we checked our windows, but nothing had moved. It was November 2, 1942. It seemed Uncle Karl and Aunt Luise were quite excited about us wanting another baby, so they played along.

Mom sent me to Aunt Elisabeth to pick up some yarn, and on the way home I met Uncle Karl. He said, "The stork was at your home, but I told him to go away to your Aunt Martha's, up the hill." I went home and checked all the windowsills and, sure enough, all the sugar was gone! We had missed the stork.

My cousin Friedel was born on that day in November.

Who Will Be The First?

Mother had a way with me, and to keep me content, she gave me a bar of soap and a bowl of water. I washed and washed until the soap was gone.

She also had a very nice radio. I was always fascinated when there was a song on the radio and she could sing the song. One day I opened the back of the radio with a screwdriver. I had the whole back open when, much to my surprise, Mom came in. She questioned me first of all as to what I was doing with a screwdriver; then she asked why I was taking the back off the radio, so I explained I wanted to see all the people inside who were singing.

Our toilet was on the other side of the house, one toilet for two families, so a night-throne (potty) was a very important piece of our belongings. Just before going to bed, we were all sent to the toilet. During wintertime, when it was dark and cold, going to the toilet was even more complicated. Many times we children did not want to go. My sister was very much afraid of the dark, so if during the day my sister and I had a quarrel, I only needed to say to her, "I will not go to the toilet with you," and she would cry.

Sometimes we raced to the toilet and often we arrived together, so we all squeezed on the toilet together, one in front and two on the side. One night Uncle Karl, the landlord, stayed at home with us while the women went to a revival meeting on a nice summer day. Mother had put us to bed and locked the door, but left the key on the outside of the door with Uncle Karl in charge.

My brother, Guenter, needed to go to the toilet, and we decided to take a different route. Instead of using the potty under the bed, we cut up a piece of cardboard and made Guenter use it. When he was done, we flung it out the window into Uncle Karl's garden. The next day Mom had a personal visit from Uncle Karl to discuss the incident.

Beetlebugs

I enjoyed going to school, although at times the homework was too much for a very active little girl. Mom insisted we have all our homework done before playing outside, but the grass was never tall enough to roam around in.

Mother always had flowers on the kitchen table. Quite often it was a bouquet of just plain grass. We had a tree house in the woods where we gathered all kinds of bugs, especially the beetlebug. These were so plentiful in the spring! We children would kick a tree and the beetles would fall down to the ground, then we collected the beetles in large tin cans with a lid on.

Once all of us children came home with a good supply of beetlebugs. We were so excited and wanted to show our mother our collection. Before Mom could say a word, we opened our tin cans. Suddenly, our kitchen was as black as the night. All the cooped-up beetles came out all at once. Mother almost lost her mind! With the help of our landlady, our precious beetlebug collection was soon under control.

My homework for school the next day was an essay about the beetlebug. Usually Mother would check our homework the night before, but this time she had forgotten about it. The next morning, just before school, Mom asked me to show her my essay, which I did. Mom looked at me very seriously and said with a frown, "You will be late for school today," and late I was! You see, my essay had one sentence: "*Der Maykaefer*" (the beetle). The beetle has one trunk, two wings, and six legs."

After an hour or so, I had a story about a page long telling about the beetle being so harmful and destroying the beautiful beech trees in their younger stages. My brother also wrote an essay which had to do with a green lawn, a most wonderful way to describe the grass. He began by telling how it would spread, almost like being "boastful," because it would grow everywhere.

Mother was a good teacher. She explained things to us and taught us to read and write. Plus, she would spend time with us and played with us. She could also play the guitar and could sing. With her help, I learned to put my fingers on the right guitar strings, then she would sing for me so I could learn chords and how to harmonize.

The Ruby Red Pitcher

My father had sent us different packages. Each of us children received a pair of rubber boots and many cans of Norwegian sardines, which were very delicious in a time of need.

Mom received a beautiful lamb jacket, a pair of leather boots, a cap, and mittens made from goat's hair. She looked so great in this outfit that people turned their heads to look at her.

In one of the packages was a ruby red pitcher—ruby red on the outside and all white on the inside. It was beautiful.

Quite a few years had passed since my hand accident so I wanted to get our milk in this pretty pitcher. I was now eight years old and could be trusted with such a priceless possession, but Mom said, "No, Christel."

Every day I was assigned to get the milk from the dairy, but I was tired of always getting the milk in the same pot, so after a while I asked again, begging Mother to let me have the pitcher just one time only. Mom looked at me and said, "Okay, Christel, one time."

I was so proud! I walked the main road so people would ask me about the very pretty ruby red pitcher, and people did ask. I got the milk and was walking across the schoolyard when my hand just opened up all by itself, and suddenly the ruby red pitcher with spilled milk lay before me! To this day I do not know how I ever was able to walk home to tell Mom about the pitcher.

I remember Mother going in the bedroom. I do not know what I would have done. I wonder if Mom was afraid that I would fall again and cut my hand or disappointed about her precious pitcher?

Burning House

Mom could make very quick decisions. She would say, "Children, get ready. We are going shopping." We would take a train ride to another town or walk. If the weather was nice, it was always a pleasure to walk with Mom through the hills. She would sing and we marched to her tune. Sometimes we walked one way, then if we had a lot to carry we took the train or bus back.

One trip Mom took with us was in late fall. We had come on the five o'clock train when Mom heard someone say, "There was a fire in town!" Mom turned around and asked the person behind her where the fire was, and he said, "Maybe your house!"

Mom almost left us kids behind because she started going faster, then began to run. We all ran, as well, although we did not have very far to go. We were living near the fire station—actually, right next door. As we came around the corner, we saw the firemen holding hoses and spraying the barn and other houses. The house was a Fachwerk house, which had been built between 1600 and 1700 and was under protection of the government.

The fire had started in the chimney and was kept at bay because of the fast-acting firemen and the location of the fire truck.

It was late one night during harvest time, and Mom was still reading a book when she noticed a flickering light. She did not take too much notice until it was not just flickering but a steady light, and still it was different. As she leaned from the window, she saw the threshing machine and the sawmill in flames.

She grabbed her dress, threw it over herself, and ran through the house, alarming the landlord. With neighbors she ran through the town yelling, "FIRE!" There were no telephones, so everything went from mouth to mouth. It took a while, but many townspeople helped by carrying buckets of water and dousing the fire until the fire truck arrived. It was quite a loss, because people needed the threshing machine at the time of harvest and had to find someone else's machine.

During the war, the farmers had to give one-tenth of their harvest to the government. The owner of the threshing machine or combine was in charge of ensuring the one-tenth was first taken out. If there were ten sacks of wheat harvested, one had to be delivered to the town barn.

I recall one time our landlord gave the grain a good whipping before he took it to be threshed, and the threshing machine operator said, "Oh, my. You had a lot of birds getting into your wheat." No one said another word.

If the farmers had chickens and ten eggs, one egg had to be given to the government. The same with the milk. It was illegal to make your own butter, but all the farmers knew how to do it and they did.

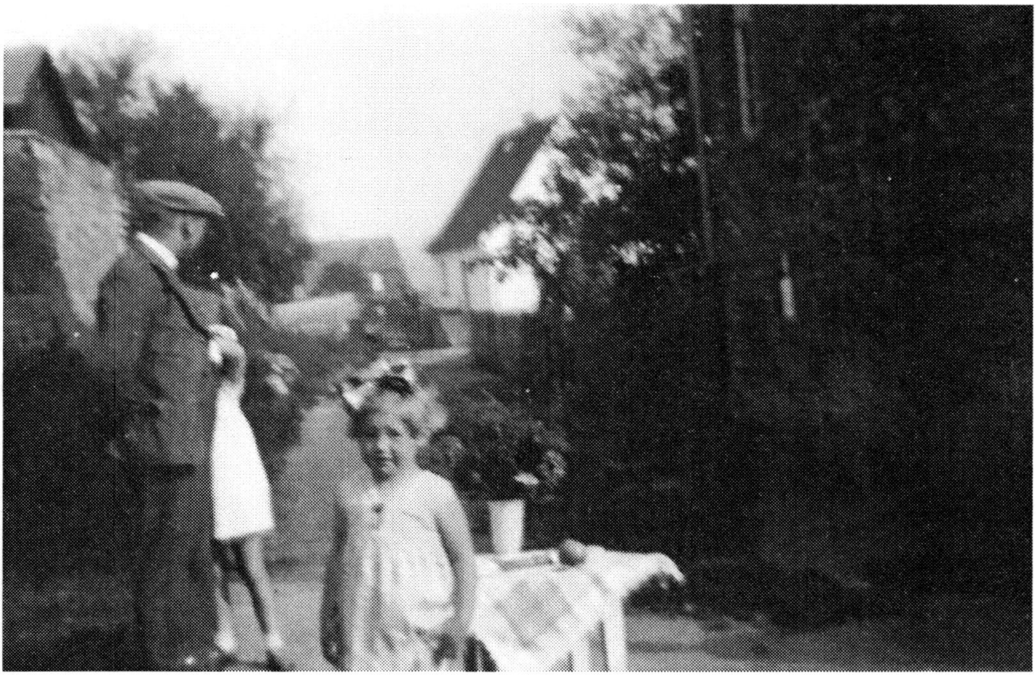

Summer

Playing in the sun, playing house, and serving food and tea on small dishes were some of my fondest memories.

Sometimes it was so very hot, and our bedroom was right under the roof and did not cool down.

We had the joy of going swimming during the day. Mom and some other older ladies went into the water late at night, especially after making hay, digging up potatoes, or harvesting wheat.

Grandfather used to be a skipper on a ship on the Atlantic Ocean, so Mom was born near the water but never learned how to swim. Grandpa's remark was, "You only get in the water when you know how to swim." The whole family, five girls, moved inland so the ocean only became a dream in later years.

Mom was very eager to take us to the water, a river, which ran through the valley near our town. She wanted us children to learn to swim, and that we did. The community swimming hole was about fifteen minutes away from our home if we used the shortcut over the railroad tracks and through the farmer's grass field. The farmer complained and it was closed off, but someone would find and make another trail.

We could see our bedroom window from the water hole, and when it was time to go home Mom would hang out a towel. After a while, some children used that signal as well, although others used to watch the train. Around 5 P.M. there were two trains coming to bring the workers and students home. Sometimes Mom would say, "When the second train comes, get ready and come home." It really worked well for many children. If the wind would blow a certain way, we could count the chimes on the church clock, since it was a luxury to have a watch.

Childhood Days

At a very early age I attended the town's daycare center. I wanted my sister to go as well for companionship, but Mom thought she was too young and that it was a long way for her little legs. I was just a year older, so Mom did a little investigating. She had asked some people who lived on the way to the daycare to encourage us on our journey. Mom could see us going up that steep hill, almost to the building, but in case we lingered she wanted a friendly face to tell us to hurry up.

Mom would travel that road in fifteen minutes, but we could easily use up an hour. We had people come out of their homes to tell us to hurry up. Sometimes we needed a drink of water first before traveling on.

On the way home, near a steep bank, there was an anthill with large carpenter ants. We little ones were told they were very tasty and we should catch some and put their hind ends against our mouths and squeeze hard and a sour-tasting liquid squirted into our mouths!

On that same street lived a man who had a grocery and a shoe store. He was very big and had a very big, protruding belly. The townspeople called him Big Fat Delmes. My sister and I and two neighbor boys were going to play Fat Delmes, so we had stuffed pillows under our pants and dresses. As we were yelling and acting out, he came charging out of his store and got hold of one of the boys. Very annoyed, he said, "Children, who am I and what is my name?" Out of all our mouths came, "You are Mr. Benner!" He had a big smile on his face and seemed to be very glad that we knew his real name.

Scream Louder

Mother was pregnant with my brother Guenter, who was to be born in October. Oma Lina Decker called on my mother to help with harvesting wheat or rye. It was a very hot August day in 1939 and the walk to the field was already exasperating. Walking on a rocky road in the middle of the day took a lot out of my mother, plus being pregnant and having a three-year-old walking beside her, which was a lot for anyone. Just getting to the field was a job well done, according to Mom.

There was not a tree in sight, so I sat on the side of the field in the hot noonday sun. After a while I started to cry and cry. Mother came to comfort me, but eventually I became more uncomfortable. When Mom came by again to check on me, she told me, "Cry louder!" So I screamed at the top of my lungs until Grandma Lina said, "Minna, take that child and go home."

Mother only needed to be told once and she was headed for home. Well, I guess I saved her that day.

Wash Days

It was on Mondays when Mother got the washing done. We had to use the landlord's basement kitchen, which had a concrete floor and was used in the summer by the landlord's family because it was nice and cool. They kept it heated in the winter using a flattop oven. Warm food was mixed on the stove for the animals, which were just next door. The animals—two cows, a pig or two, and chickens, we all lived under one roof to save energy.

A little farm was a Godsend during the war. Butchering was done in the fall, then ham, meats, and sausages were smoked and cured. It was a feast on the day of butchering, but not nice to look at. We children were kept at bay but were able to have a good meal with sauerkraut, fresh potatoes, and ribs as well as homemade sausages.

It was a tradition in our town to find out who had butchered. The children would then go to the house, holding a long stick with a container on the end that reached through a window. The container was then filled with sauerkraut and ribs.

It was easier to do the laundry in the summer, although Mother had to ask when she was able to use the basement kitchen. It was every four to six weeks when wash day came around.

Now I know how hard it must have been for her to wash by hand. She used a washboard or a plunger and she was always bent over, reaching down to use the plunger or the board. There was no laundry soap like we have now. Instead, a bar of Ivory soap was put into a large, copper kettle that could be heated.

The whites (sheets and covers) were then put into the copper kettle and slowly heated to just before the boiling point, then simmered and turned for about thirty to forty minutes. With a long wooden spoon, the hot laundry was then pulled out into a container of cold water for rinsing. If the sun was shining, Mom would place the white linen on grass for the sun to bleach out the stains. She left us children with a container full of water to sprinkle the linen to keep it wet, for it should not get dry. She also told us not to leave shoe prints on the now white linen.

In the meantime, Mom would wash the lighter-colored clothes with a plunger using the water from the copper kettle. Then she would rinse the colored clothes to be hung up to dry, usually in the attic, although the white clothes were hung outside on the wash line. Socks and pants were all scrubbed by hand.

The wash day schedule went like this: Monday–wash, Tuesday–dry, Wednesday–iron, and Thursday–mend.

It was on one of those hot summer days that we had a real scare. Mother had hung up all the clothes in the attic to dry. A thunderstorm was brewing, and everyone was in the basement kitchen when a low-flying airplane came over our house and shot at us. We all rushed into the cellar. Somehow we had not heard the siren, so we all had a very scary surprise! Later on, when Mother had checked on the laundry in the attic, she noticed that the bullets had gone through many of our clothes, which were then rendered useless.

The Town Blackboard

The town hall had a very large blackboard which hung in the center of town. Anyone caught stealing had his or her name written on the blackboard. Early in the morning, people would go to read the names. It was like a newspaper.

For town news to be made known there was a bellman, and certain places had a wooden board. The bellman would ring his bell when he had posted the town news. To me, it always was very interesting to read the news of the day, especially once I knew how to read.

My friend, Louise, and I were way out in the hills one day when we discovered some apple and pear trees. We stuffed our pockets when someone hollered at us that we were stealing someone's fruit and he was going to report it to the police.

Louise and I ran as fast as we could, dropping all the fruit as we ran home. At home, I stood behind the window, waiting for the police to come by at any moment. I did not tell Mother, thus I nursed a very bad deed for a while. I wanted to know if my name was on that blackboard. The next day, Mom (who knew that something was not quite right) walked with me to the blackboard, but it was blank.

The Bracelet

It was a cold winter morning before school, and I must have been in the fourth grade. All the different grades had to line up at the school entrance. If there was an announcement, that was the time when all the classes were together in one place. Lost and found items, dismissals from certain classes, or changes of teachers were announced.

Usually the teachers called for the younger grades first, but on this day a teacher held up a bracelet that had been found in the snow. The teacher held it very high for everyone to see, but nobody claimed it. So I raised my hand, and the bracelet was given to me. It did not belong to me so I could not wear it, for Mother would have noticed. Instead, I tucked it away inside of my mother's guitar, then totally forgot about it.

Just before Christmas, a relative wanted to borrow Mom's guitar, but they couldn't even play it and returned it quite quickly, telling her what was found inside the guitar. It was all very funny at first, but then it became a very serious matter. Mom wanted to know who did this and all three of us children acted very innocent, like the fresh, clean, driven snow.

So Mom had a job on her hands, for I was not about to confess to something that had happened so long ago, in my own mind. Besides, surely the statue of limitations had passed, so I thought. My mother's thinking was the godly way—confess thy sins and thou shall be forgiven. All three of us children were punished hard with a rod. I dug myself in deeper and deeper by not confessing, and there seemed to be no way out.

Mom was persistent. She stopped talking to us, feeding us without uttering a word. This was worse than a good licking. Help arrived when our landlady came and tucked us into bed, and she asked us to tell her who did it.

My sister finally said she did it just to get it over with. But Mother knew better. The whole thing lasted a week. It was on a Monday morning when I came running home to tell Mother about a conference in school she had to attend. She looked at me with her big brown eyes, and I think now she looked at me with the eyes of the Lord, so penetrating I could not resist telling her the truth. And woe again, the rod of Aaron was placed on my behind. But it was an inner healing I had longed for the last few days. Confession is good for the soul!

I returned the bracelet to the school office but was never able to find out about the true owner until fifty years later. My father had died and we had gathered afterwards with old schoolmates. Stories were being told about the good old times when I mentioned the bracelet and how I obtained it. Gudrun, a distant relative, said, "Christel, what is this about a bracelet?"

I was eager to tell it again when she looked at me and said, "Christel, that was my bracelet." I was stunned and in awe. Gudrun had always wondered what happened to her bracelet, which was a gift from England from her dad. She had asked her mother if she could wear the bracelet to school—just once—and her mom said, "No, only to church." Gudrun disobeyed and lost it. She was never able to tell her mother and always wondered about her lost bracelet. After so many years, we forgave each other and I sent her one of my arm bracelets from Alaska.

May 1945

It was May when the war came to an end. Many tanks and trucks came through our town, but they were all German soldiers and as mom explained that the war was over and they were about to be captured.

Many things and actions we children did not understand. Somehow there was great excitement. People were out on the streets and hanging from windows. Mom had a sheet hanging from the side of our home. At times, she would tell us to keep our hands on the side and not point. She was afraid that it might look like a gun.

We were told that foreign soldiers with tanks had invaded the town. We knew it was true because these men wore different uniforms. Some of the soldiers were black and spoke a different language. They came like flies and many went through our home. By evening, we counted twenty-six men in uniform who had come through our home searching for German soldiers.

The whole town buzzed like a beehive being disturbed. There were soldiers everywhere, including our home. Mother followed them from the attic, to the bedroom, to the kitchen, and then the living room. Some soldier turned over photos of my dad and opened drawers. Mom did not let them out of her sight.

Soldiers came, while others went, which went on for days. Our school was turned into a US headquarters, which also had a first aid station.

One morning about 4 A.M., someone knocked on our bedroom door. We three children were all in bed with Mother when four servicemen entered and wanted to see my mom's passport. "No passport in bed," she said, motioning to them with her hands. We all drew closer to Mom when she said, "Christel, get up and hand me my little wooden box from the closet."

Mother had all kinds of photos and letters from my dad in there and also her passport. The men, who carried flashlights, looked very closely at the passport then handed it back to Mom and left. Mom was in utter dismay, but we all heard the men leave. It was the hand of the Lord who protected my mother from all evil.

The soldiers were still coming around days after, so our landlord hung up the sign from when we had diphtheria in our home. The sign read PLEASE STAY AWAY—DIPHTHERIA IN THE HOUSE.

Well, that did the trick. When the servicemen saw the sign, they held their arms in front of them and left.

Mom must have known about all this because she dug a big hole in the ground at the cemetery and buried my father's stuff. She also had a big bucket with paint and changed the color of the uniforms my dad left behind. Anything that looked valuable she put in boxes she buried in the ground for safekeeping, and she walked with every soldier through the house.

My little brother, Guenter, who was about six years old at the time, had a wooden gun and was hiding in the basement behind some straw when a soldier came through. Guenter moved from his hiding place and in a split second the soldier turned, held the gun toward my brother, and aimed.

Guenter crawled from his corner and the soldier just motioned toward my mother, waving his hand. "Little boy…does not matter."

Nobody was to leave the house without proper identification. A passport had to be carried at all times without exception. Curfew was set for all the citizens. We had to be in by ten at night and stay in until seven in the morning. No one was to be seen on the streets.

All of us children were used to saying "Heil Hitler" to everyone we met. Now we were told to say, "Guten Tag" for good day, "Guten Morgen" for good morning, or "Guten Abend" for good evening. Every day new rules were laid out. Changes were plentiful. Mother claimed Hebrews 12: *"We have a cloud of witnesses surrounding us."*

We children had not seen a black person before. When all the soldiers came, there were black people among them, and somehow a rumor went through town that the blacks would bite every woman on the legs who did not wear socks. When I first saw black people, I can remember their beautiful white teeth. Now we were told they would bite females on the legs.

I remember running home and telling mother to please put long socks on. Mom was very upset about the rumor and explained about the people from Africa, giving us children a history and geography lesson.

Mother sent me to run errands for her and as I walked along the street, I made room for a large pickup. To my excitement, a crate of oranges fell off the truck. People and children came from all corners to pick up the golden yellow fruit, which I had never seen before. I grabbed one orange and ran home with it, and Mom's eyes became wide as she asked me about the fruit. We shared that one orange with two families.

Our garden was our home away from home. Mom made us pick weeds, and during harvest time we picked what was available.

It was one of those great days in the garden when mother noticed a stranger watching us from under one of the trees nearby. He waved to me and, not knowing what to do, I saw Mother nodding for me to go and see. He could not speak German so we concluded he was an American soldier. He handed me a large bag full of candies, which was almost unbelievable. I had never seen so many different candies.

I ran back. Then he waved back to us and disappeared. Talk about Christmas in summer!

Mother attended a church meeting with some other people in a nearby town. It was later than they thought when all of them had to walk home. No one talked as they walked along a main highway. In the near distance, they heard a truck coming closer. They tried to get out of the light, but all of them were caught. US servicemen surrounded them, holding flashlights and asking questions. "Passport," said one of them.

Some of the people in Mom's group had IDs around their necks, but Mom couldn't find her ID. After a lot of commotion, she gave her name and address and was told to pay 100 DM ($100) or go to jail for one week. I still remember her telling us of her choice to go to jail or pay money we didn't have.

"Mother, please don't go to jail. We won't eat for the next month," was our plea. Somehow she paid that money, doing extra chores for the community, such as cleaning out the town's bull stable and cutting their hay for the winter.

CHURCH EXTENSION PLAN

Partners in Ministry

Toll-free 1-800-821-1112   *Web site* http://www.cepnet.com

Winter Wonderland

We were all still in bed when Mother said, "Children, we have snow!" Oh my, we were out of bed very quickly, ready to test the firmness of the beautiful, white, fluffy stuff.

How did Mom know? We were still in bed. The horse-driven snow plow with the bells ringing let the people know. The driver would go up and down the main streets and the residents had to clean their walkways by seven o'clock in the morning. It was just plain fun to move the snow away from stairs and sidewalks. Often I found myself praying for snow, because without it we had no winter. Christmas without snow was unthinkable!

I think we always had snow when I was growing up. One thing I remember: we were always cold. The girls only had dresses to wear. Mom knitted our stockings, and they were so itchy and scratchy one could barely sit still. Plus we would grow out of them so quickly so that the upper legs would be bare. So we hoped our winter coats would cover what needed to be covered.

My cousin Trude once received a long, wooly, red coat, and I wanted it. One day I walked up to their home and asked Aunt Martha if I could have Trude's red coat. Aunt Martha said, "When Trude is no more, then you can have it." Well, Trude did not die. In fact, at the time of this writing, she is still alive.

Our school class was having an outing. We were going to do some sledding down the mountain, and I wanted some pants to wear. In desperation, I went up to the attic and checked out my father's pants, which were kept in mothballs until his return from the war. I saw a gray pair and tried them on. Oh my, I had some work to do. Safety pins became my tools. The hems were fastened with pins. It seemed impossible to use a belt, but that was the only thing I had. The belt went several times around my waist to secure the pants, then a dress over the pants, and finally a coat. Surely I looked like a barrel, but I was warm.

We were able to go to church again without interruption. Aunt Maria was the Sunday school teacher during the Hitler regime. A Nazi was present who was to give the message, but was unable to control all the children so he told Aunt Maria to carry on. And now we had freedom to preach God's Word. Aunt Maria had found her calling.

My mother and Aunt Elisabeth were the Sunday school helpers. Quite often they counted over one hundred children. Aunt Maria had never married but she was the aunt for many children in town.

When Christmas came around, the whole town participated in the Christmas story. All us children had to learn parts. I recall going to practices ever so often. It was so festive, going through fresh snow. We were very eager learning our parts, whether they be as Mary or Joseph or the innkeeper. Dressing up was the most exciting occurrence. We all wanted to be angels. Long poems and songs were memorized, and Mother would encourage us and listen.

Advent Time

We had one sled, one pair of skis, and one pair of ice skates for three children. I had trouble with the sizes, so the shoes for the skis and ice skates never fit me. They were always too small, so I never did learn to ski or ice skate. But when it came to sledding down the mountains, we were all kings.

Some of the hills were so steep we only had time to make one run before it got too dark. Otherwise we could have lost our way. The only lights we could see were the streetlights, and during the war there were no lights at all.

Advent time—the time before Christmas—is four weeks. A wreath from spruce and fir was made and hung up in almost every home. Churches and community halls had special bazaars where people would gather and buy ornaments. Wreaths were also made with red ribbons and four large candles. The first candle was lit four weeks before Christmas and one was added every week. The preachers would preach about the announcement of Jesus' birth. We also sang pre-Christmas songs. Everything was so very secretive. Some people would start going to church, a once-a-year occurrence.

During Hitler's reign, all Christmas songs were illegal to sing. Instead, regular folk songs were sung rather than Christmas songs. However, Mother continued to sing the songs of Zion, Christmas songs, and "Jesus loves me, this I know, for the Bible tells me so...."

Es Weihnachtet sehr (Christmas)

Mother always had made Christmas very special. There was never enough of anything, but it was festive. We always had a tree with decorations, mainly handmade.

We grew up with fairy tales and Santa Claus, and Mother told us the difference so we knew the Bible stories were true and the other tales were just make believe.

The story of Jesus' birth and about Mary and Joseph was read over and over, and we usually memorized parts from the Christmas story.

One of the boys who was eager to play the innkeeper knew about the Bible story and that his part was to say, "There is no room in the inn. Go away!" But when he saw Mary and Joseph in his very childish way he instead said, "Come to my place. It is cold out there. I will give you my bed!"

Singing with Mom was a delight. She knew all the words and made us memorize them. "Children," she said, "tomorrow is Christmas. I want you to stay in bed until you hear the Christmas bell coming from the living room." We could hardly wait.

It was early morning. We heard bells coming from the outside because fresh fallen snow was plowed off the streets with horse-pulled sleighs. The sleighs had storm lights all around, so everything glistened. It looked so very pretty. Winter wonderland was in the making. It was not quite light, but Mother was already up and tending to the fire, getting wood and coals. We did not need the stove to cook breakfast on since a slice of bread and a cup of milk was our meal. Or would it be different today because of Christmas?

It was very quiet in the house, so still it was eerie.

Mom had a way to get the right Christmas present for herself. She needed a petticoat, so she went to the store and purchased the petticoat. Then she sent us children to that same department store and had the clerk persuade us to buy this petticoat, and she was elated because this was what she really needed.

Mom would also give us some small change to buy something for each other. I remember one year we bought glitter for the tree.

We were wondering what we would find under the tree. Guenter would have his red little car fixed again. My doll would have brand new eyes and her arm fixed. Inge's dollhouse lacked furniture, so there might be a tiny little chair and a table. We had to wait, but not too long anymore. The bell would be ringing soon. But listen—did you hear something? Yes, it was a bell. Yes, there were three distinct rings. We opened the door just a little to peek into our living room. We saw lights, but what we saw was heavenly. Was it an angel or the Christ child with glitter in his hair? We three children had never, ever seen anything like that. We could not move. The Christ child was turned away from us and was lighting our Christmas tree, which had real candles. It was so awesome. We watched until the being was gone. We still could hardly believe what we just saw. Everything was so quiet, even the opening and shutting of the door, which always had squeaked.

Oh my, we were alone. The tree was lit. There were presents under the tree and apples, nuts, and cookies. We were rich!

Just then the door opened and Mom came in with an armload of wood. We just talked all together, telling her what we had just experienced. Mom stood and listened with tears in her eyes because she saw us little ones so very happy.

That morning we had real white bread, butter, and real strawberry jam for breakfast. Then there were our presents, a ball to play with, a pair of boots, an umbrella, and a rain jacket.

Mom was always satisfied with whatever she received. Earlier in the month, Mom had received a package from dad: a fur jacket, boots, and accessories.

We felt blessed. We had good gifts, a nice breakfast, and each other.

Oh, Christmas Tree

Mom saw to it that we always had a tree, and to this day I enjoy a spruce tree.

Mom told us the story about three trees in the middle of the forest and how each tree was very special. This was a favorite Christmas story to hear at bedtime.

"You see, each tree wanted to serve the Creator of the universe in a different way. One tree said to the other, 'All I want to do is stay right here and be a testimony to the other trees.'

"'Oh, that is very good,' said the second tree. 'And I will be a home for many birds.'

"The third tree said, 'I'd like to see the world.'

"It was so peaceful in the woods. One could hear children in the distance. Snow was falling, and the three trees all received a white overcoat. The trees did not feel the cold and so they thanked the Lord.

"It was early in the morning when the trees heard loud voices in the distance and axes chopping and chains rattling. One of the trees said, 'I can see men coming up the hill and talking to each other.'

"'What are they saying?' asked the second tree.

"'They are talking about cutting down some trees.'

"'Oh,' the tree said, 'I suddenly feel so cold. I am chilled down to my trunk.' The other trees felt the same, and they were scared. Then the trees could hear the sound of saws and axes again.

"'What is this? I am shaking. What are these men doing to me?' Two of the trees were cut down and loaded up on a big cart. A long journey lay ahead of them. The trees were loaded and reloaded, then separated and each went on its way."

The next night, Mom would continue with the story....

"The first tree tried to think back to its younger years. *Yes, I have grown and been made into something useful. The birds in the air found different places to nest, I'm sure. Now I'm here to hold feed for some animals.*

"*Tonight has been very restless. The animals could not sleep. Something was different. The young couple in the corner was very quiet, but not for long. Something is happening! I can't figure out what.* The tree listened. *I hear a baby cry, but how could this be? Is it coming from the outside or from the stable?*

"The man said to the young lady, 'Mary, it's a boy.' In a very weak voice she answered, 'Oh, Joseph, the Word has come true.'

"Joseph found the manger in a corner and that was where they laid the tiny little baby. The little tree became so excited. *First I gave the birds a home; now I am holding a baby, and I think he is a very special one.* The tree heard Mary say, 'What a pretty manger, Joseph. Our baby will be warm.' The little tree was not lonely anymore and felt very important.

"Now, off to bed," Mother would say. "We will talk about the other two trees later."

Just before bedtime the next night, Mother began:

"The second tree journeyed through many harbors, was loaded onto barges, and then tied down in the water with many other trees. This was very exciting, since this tree wanted to travel and see the world. The tree was so waterlogged, plus stripped of all its branches, feeling naked and cold. Still, the tree praised the Creator.

"Months and years went by. One day a very big ship came by and all the logs were loaded on it. A very long journey lay ahead. The day came when the logs were unloaded and different buyers bid on them. 'Oh, please, Creator, make something good out of me,' the tree prayed.

"Men came and looked at the wood, talked amongst themselves, and pointed to different trees, including the second tree. The trees were loaded and unloaded again. *I heard a man named Peter wanted to build a boat, as well as some other names.* The second tree was excited. *I will travel on the water. I will carry people from shore to shore.*

"The men who worked on the boat were very knowledgeable and it was not long before the boat was finished. *I heard them call the boat 'Peter's Boat'.*

"Sometime later, they were in a very bad storm. Peter and his men saw a ghost walking on the water. The tree heard the men yelling and screaming, 'Who is this, who is there?'

"Then the tree heard the voice say, 'It is I, Jesus.'

"Peter recognized the voice and yelled, 'Jesus, if it is you, let me come to you on the water.'

"Jesus answered, 'Peter, come.' The tree saw Peter step on the water and he did not sink. This was a miracle. Suddenly, Peter called, 'Lord, I am sinking.' Jesus pulled him out of the water. Then the tree knew. *Jesus is the Son of God!*"

It was cold, snowy, and dark outside, so after supper we all wanted to know what happened to the third tree.

"Often the tree wondered about the other two trees. The third tree had not been cut down but allowed to stay in the forest to grow tall. The tree hoped it could stay forever on this spot, praising the Lord. Its branches reached high to the heavens.

"All the snow had melted. Spring was in the air, and the birds were making nests. Deer were having their young ones. There was a lot of activity now in the woods. On Sunday, people came enjoying a walk in the fresh air and sunshine.

"It was late one afternoon when some men came and put an orange ribbon around the tree's trunk. Not long after that, it was cut down and loaded on a big cart and shipped far away. It heard some people say, 'All these logs are going to be shipped to the Holy Land.'

"This was so. The trees were sold in Jerusalem for a special purpose. The third tree was disturbed when it heard that.

"Looking around, the tree felt lonely. 'I am going to be shipped to Jerusalem for a special purpose. Oh, Creator, stand by me,' the tree prayed.

"There were so many people and animals. The tree suddenly became very frightened. All the logs were unloaded on a special wagon in that great city by the Eastern Gate. The tree was able to look down and was aware of a clean brook close by.

"A very rough-looking man got hold of the tree when he saw the orange ribbon and just pointed without saying a word. The tree was pulled and yanked, then placed on someone's shoulder.

"The tree was too heavy for one person to carry, but men yelled and screamed louder than ever. The women and children followed. Some cried and some even threw rocks at the man who was carrying the tree on his shoulder.

"'Why me, Great Creator?' the third tree asked.

"A still, small voice replied, 'This is your special purpose.'

"The tree tried its very best to lighten the load for that man, but he fell beneath the load. What was going to happen next? The road became quite narrow and steep. Finally, everyone stopped on top of a hill. The tree saw old bones lying around. There was still some sap left in its trunk and it cried and sobbed when it was made aware of what was going to happen to the man who carried it up the hill. Those men made a cross out of the tree and nailed that man onto its trunk. He did not say a word in protest.

"Then the tree could hear Him say, 'Father, forgive them, for they know not what they do.' What a man. He died on the tree, and it heard someone from the crowd say, 'Truly He was the Son of God.'

"Then the tree was sorrowful. The Son of God. The Creator died and hung on the cross. All it could do now is look up and point the way to heaven."

My mother always was a good storyteller.

A Month of December Not to Be Forgotten

Refugees overran Germany. Our town was very kind to the ones who had to flee their homeland, East Germany, after the war. All the people in West Germany had to make room and absorb all those displaced people. Officials came around to the houses and counted rooms, then people. In addition, the homeowners were told how many people they had to take in. There were people everywhere, and the fire engines were parked outside to make room for all those many people, who also were very hungry. They had with them most of their possessions, only what they could carry. Children were bedded in carts, although some had to walk. They had come a long way and needed food, clothing, and shelter.

It was December. Snow was on the ground and we were told to move into our Grandma Lina's house, who had died in October 1950. Mother had made a visit to the townspeople very frequently, telling them we were entitled to move into my dad's house. The house we were living in had become very small with teenagers growing up. Refugees had occupied Grandma's house and we wanted it, so Mom was very persistent and determined. I guess the mayor just got very tired of Mom coming every day, then the refugees were told to find a different place and we moved in because we had no other place to go.

Mother was also the main character in a Christmas pageant, which was to be performed the day after Christmas in the gym. Because of all the moving and packing and learning her lines, she was exhausted and a nervous bundle. She had lost her voice, so singing was out. My cousin Trude, who was also to be the narrator, helped Mom practice and she sang while Mom moved her mouth. There were only a few weeks left before Christmas.

Things had become very wild while moving all our stuff during a snowstorm. We children made many trips wearing clothes on top of each other. There was no moving van, so we had to do it all by foot. It was only a half-hour walk for us children. Our landlord helped by loading our stuff on a cart and we pulled it, while a horse-drawn carriage was used to transport our furniture.

My Dad in Russia

To tell all the stories my dad had experienced in the prison camp would take a lot of time. He was taken prisoner in 1945 in Moscow, Russia, and transported to Poland for further interrogation, but had escaped with some other men. Father knew the stars and told the men to walk by night, which would be much safer, and sleep during the day. He kept the North Star on his right side during the night as they walked west, trying to get to Germany. In the winter with a full moon, it was very difficult to make out the trail. Russia and Poland are known for their harsh winters.

The men, about ten of them, tried to stay close to trees as much as possible. When they were getting near a village, they scattered. Each one was on his own to find food, then hide it or share it. Father seemed to get food from some of the people. He had to be careful, because he was a German ex-soldier, but he prayed and a host of angels walked beside him.

The group of men just walked out of the forest when Dad saw danger. He hid himself behind a very skinny bush, the others trying to hide as well, when shots were fired. Father, not knowing what happened, stayed very still for a long time. He did not dare to look up, so he fell asleep and didn't know for how long. It was a very sad picture when he finally looked up. All of the men were dead, and he was the only one who had survived. Now he was on his own, walking westward toward Germany.

Again he walked a trail, maybe made by animals or humans. It was full moon and no one was in sight, just the moon, his shadow, the Lord, and himself. He told us he could see very far into the distance when he saw something coming up on his tail. Dad's prayers were cranked up into high gear. He saw a string of humans, or what could it be? There was no place to hide—the snow was deep, but he had no time to dig a hole. These so-called humans came closer and Dad just prayed, "Lord, what do you want me to do?"

Suddenly, he heard himself whistle three times, which in normal times would have been unheard of, then he saw these people just turn around and walk away.

At a later date, my dad was captured and taken deep into Russia with many other prisoners. They were all put into cattle cars with straw to be transported and put into various camps along the way.

Men and women—Russians, Polish, and Germans alike—were all transported deep into Siberia. What were their evil deeds? Some had talked too much, some had been fighting the war, and some were disobedient. Russian women were made prostitutes and then shipped off and sent away. Christian people were doomed when they were caught preaching the Bible.

The Siberian train went for weeks and months, never empty, always with a load of helpless people. Some were left off at deserted railroad stations to help build the Siberian railroad or help repair it. Others like my dad were put into a very large camp with hundreds and hundreds of other prisoners. The winter occupation was cutting and hauling trees out of the forest, and in the summer preparing the wood for transportation.

My dad told about an older man who had no strength left, so he had asked the Lord to help him carry the big logs. It was a real blessing when Christians found other believers. In little groups they encouraged each other, prayed, and had Holy communion with so-called coffee made from grain.

That old man had an experience he told of seeing an angel on one side of his log, helping to carry it.

Dad had asked the Lord about his return to Germany. He was already in his fifth year and still no sign, but it was not very far.

It was the last month of 1950 when Father had a dream. He walked into the makeshift Russian office on the compound and saw a large list, like Santa carries around at Christmas, with names on it—names of the prisoners. He looked the list over and recognized a man's name he knew—Herbert! So Dad asked around, "Where is my name?" He was told, "Not this week, but next week." Herbert went home as Dad said, and Father came home the following week, as he was told in a dream.

The Telegram

It was Christmas Eve morning in 1950. The small town of Herborn–Seelbach, Germany, was awake. All the baking for the holy days was done in the community bake house. People drew straws and then started about 3:00 or 4:00 A.M. with baking. Each family had a certain timeframe in which to bake and also keep the fires hot. Certain wood was used, and everyone brought their own logs.

We put our name down so we were able to bake and enjoy our own baked goods. I still remember helping Mom with pulling the sled. I felt so important leaving the house in the dark so early in the morning.

For days now the Christmas tree and the carved toys, a dollhouse, and dolls were all locked in one of the secret rooms. The only way to look in it was through the keyhole. Oh my, there was a lot to imagine.

Germany was still recovering from World War II. There was little money and hardly any food, but Mother usually was able to create a most delicious dinner for us.

Fresh snow had fallen all through the night, and it was a very bitter cold day although the sun was sending its early rays across the field. From our bedroom window, the sight was awesome. The trees glittered like tinsel on a Christmas tree. It was a day forever to be remembered.

Our father, whom we had not seen in ten years, was still in a Russian prison camp. Every day we prayed for our dad to come home, and not a meal went by where we did not pray for his safe return.

It was mid-morning on Christmas Eve 1950. Mom had just finished playing *"Leise rieselt der Schnee"* ("Softly the Snow Is Falling") on the organ when we heard a hard knock on the front door, so she went down the stairs and opened the door. A man stood there, almost looking like Santa Claus himself because of all the snow. He handed her a letter, which looked quite official. The clerk kicked the snow off his boots and coat and told Mom he had a telegram for her. The telegram carrier waited for Mom to open it and, with a loud yell, she called us children to all come downstairs. She read it over and over. The clerk needed a signature and waited and enjoyed the commotion. Finally, Mom read it very slowly: "I am on my way home. I arrive by train January 1, 1951, at 4 P.M. in Herborn. Love, Oskar."

The message of my dad's homecoming went like wildfire through the community. All the Christmas songs and the story of Christmas came alive.

The news changed Mom. She had more enthusiasm for everything, including her acting role in the play, "The Last White Rose," which was coming up. Her energy soared, and we children received a new mother. Friends and neighbors celebrated with us.

Packages of food were left at the doorstep from well wishers. The week that followed the arrival of the news was full of expectations and happiness. Mother walked on air. She searched for her old love letters and pictures. We children practiced the name "Papa." My brother, Guenter, thought Dad had golden eyes.

In his younger years, his peers called Dad "Sunday" because he was always dressed for Sunday. Mom would tell us he never drank old, warm coffee, he didn't like leftovers for dinner, and he never would walk through a puddle, so his shoes were always shiny. According to my mother, we had the most perfect father!

Suits, socks, shirts, and pants that been stored in the attic for almost ten years were hung out on the clotheslines to air out. The old grandfather clock in the corner of the living room kept on ticking, when finally the old year had come to an end at midnight. All the bells in Germany began to ring the old year out and the new year in.

All us children stayed up to celebrate. The town's choir gathered in front of our home and sang to us. We felt jubilee and excitement. In a few hours we would meet our most wonderful dad.

Mom had received a letter from city hall to appear in a timely manner to present all the paperwork about my dad's involvement as a Nazi member during the war.

Mom was shocked. She had no paperwork. It was even before they had gotten married that he had severed all strings to the party, but Mom had to come up with proof.

A meeting was set up and Mom just said, "I would like to see my husband's name on **your** list." The search went on but my dad's name did not come up. Therefore, Mom had everything resolved before Dad came home to German soil.

Dad's Arrival

The time had come for Dad's arrival. We children we going to pick him up in the nearby town. We had told Mom to stay at home and that we were capable of finding him. Oh my, we were thoughtless!

Somehow Mom agreed to this idea. When it was time, she seated us in the front part of the train. What we didn't know was she was also on the train to keep an eye on us. We started looking for our dad as soon as the train arrived at the station.

I was thirteen years old, my sister was twelve, and Guenter was eleven. Many people were at the station. We all held hands so we wouldn't get separated. How were we going to find our Dad? It almost seemed impossible to recognize a man we hardly knew.

I became aware of a group of people who were pointing toward us. Someone said, "Oskar, there are your children." A tall man with a long overcoat and a wide-rimmed hat looked at me (although it seemed through me). I guess he was looking for smaller children. Finally it dawned on me that this must be our dad.

Now as I think over that moment, I wonder what Dad thought since Mom wasn't with us?

Someone escorted us back to the train. We were all sitting in one row when I noticed my Mother behind us. She was wearing her most beautiful white lamb fur jacket and cap, knee-high boots, and gloves made from goat's hair. It was the outfit Dad had sent her from Norway. Love sparks were flying! Dad had noticed Mom. Soon both were wrapped in each other's arms. It was so wonderful. For the first time in our lives, we saw Mom and Dad holding each other.

Mom had planned an escape route to dodge the many people at the railway station in our hometown, so they left the train on the opposite side.

What a celebration for us—we had our dad home!

There's a Man in the House

Now there was a man in the house. I must admit, it was strange even calling him Father or Papa.

Food was on his mind day and night. When he arrived at the German border, all the soldiers were given a bath and personal hygiene. All the "body critters" were dealt with quite radically. Father said that fleas, bed bugs, lice, and mosquitoes had invaded Russia.

Fifty DM ($50) was given to each person, and they were told to buy whatever they wished. The only thing available were cigarettes and candies, so father brought home 50 DM worth of candies, since he was a non-smoker. His daily diet had been watery soup and a hunk of bread.

Father did not look thin to us, but what we saw was a body full of fluid. His upper lip was so thick it protruded out like a wasp had stung him. I recall at the dinner table, Dad would reach out his hands and scoop up everything edible. Mom just said, "Oskar, we are hungry as well."

Father had a very hard time adjusting. Many marriages had broken up. I overheard Mom say, "Oskar, you have to change. We did not come to you, but you came to us."

Mom and Dad could pray together and I think that was the glue of their marriage. The prayer of a righteous man availeth much. Germany was soon rebuilt and food became more plentiful.

Father stayed at home for a year, although by law, the last employer had to rehire the men who returned home from the war.

Moving

Father wanted to improve himself, so he moved to a different town for intensive training in a large newspaper printing establishment. It was a much faster pace than he was used to and his training area was in a medical department, so he learned to write and type in Latin.

Our house was divided. Mom stayed home and all us children were gone, working someplace. A job opened up near Duesseldorf, so my dad was very much interested. The pay would be good and he would look for a home for our family to move into. My parents were also very interested in having a good church nearby. The Lord was at work and in no time we all moved to Velbert. My sister and I worked in the hospital nearby, where we had room and board.

Our home was small, an upstairs with two rooms, and no water. There was a toilet with no flush. We had to go through someone's apartment to get water and then go downstairs to dump it, but no one complained. Mother prayed for us to get water in the kitchen, although the landlord said, "There is no water line under your quarters. All the lines are on the other side of the house." Mom still continued to pray for water. It was one of those severe winters in 1955 when mother heard a big yell coming from downstairs. The whole basement was underwater. A buried, dead waterline had busted exactly under our kitchen. The landlady only said, "We have been living here for twenty years and we were not aware of the waterline." In no time my dad and brother had a water line up to the sink in the kitchen.

Praise ye the Lord.

A New House, Bigger and Better

My father was a dedicated churchgoer. He walked, many times an hour each way. This was too much walking for Mom, so she and us teenagers waited for the bus, depending on the weather, which could be very severe in the winter.

We needed a car, and Father had not gotten a driver's license yet. Cars were slowly coming in.

Germany had good transportation, with train stations in every town and city, and larger cities were blessed with underground trains, 'S' trains above and underground. We had busses and streetcars and also ferry transports across rivers and lakes.

There was never enough money for a car, but Father ventured out to get his driver's license, and proud he was. Mom started praying for a black Mercedes. Her relationship with God was great, because we purchased a car that was black, and our second car was a Mercedes.

Dad still walked a lot, using the car mainly for work, to take Mom shopping, some Sunday driving to church and for sightseeing.

One lovely summer night, Dad walked home from a Bible study and prayer meeting. A shortcut was through the park, but something made him walk the main road. He passed several very large houses which could have been built by the same architect. He passed one of the houses which had three different entrances. There were two side entries, one on either side, and another entry in front of the middle part of the house. There were three different landlords, and each part had a first, second, and third floor. Eight families could live in that house.

As father passed that first part of the house, an inner voice told him he would be living there very soon. He just muttered as he passed by, "Impossible!"

As he came home, Mom handed my dad a telephone number with the request to call as soon as possible. Dad called and paid a visit to those people and found out they were owners of that one side of the building.

The House on the Poststreet

My parents were past fifty years old when we moved in with those five older ladies who never married. The sisters occupied all the upstairs, while another older couple who was childless lived in a studio apartment just under the attic. Our family of five occupied the lower floor. Our job was to keep the outside nice and clean, the garden hedge trimmed, and the snow kept at bay. The snow had to be cleared on our side of the street before 7 A.M. on weekdays for the traveling folks to reach their destination, bus, train, or workplace.

Before us children, still at home and in our teenage years, were leaving the house, Mom would advise us about the snow removal. On weekends we had to sweep the sidewalk and clean the steps to our entry, the porch, and the hallway. This was our responsibility as self-made landlords.

The sisters kept their stairs clean, but the smell and the crowing of roosters in the mornings was something else. They owned chickens and a rooster for each chicken, with a remark from them that they all had a joyless youth and would like to see the chickens happy.

The chicken house was inside the house on the way to the cellar. The chickens and roosters were led outside in a fenced-in garden, and the eggs were collected any time of the day. The youngest of the sisters, who was in her sixtieth year, was in charge of cleaning the chicken house and choosing the right chicken or rooster for the meals. She had named them all, and it seemed the poultry family listened to her callings. I still remember her coming into our living room with a chicken in her arms, petting it and telling my mom that this chicken's head was soon to come off. After that episode, Mom could not eat or even taste chicken.

One year for Christmas I had Mom persuaded to make a turkey for dinner. I knew from past experience that they were all nice and clean and all the guts were taken out. So we got one, and I told Mom to put it in the oven just as it came. Because of her being skirmish about all poultry, she followed my orders and just put it in the oven. It was not very long and our house smelled, not like cooked turkey, but like something very rotten. The turkey had not been cleaned—all the guts were left in, so we had cooked innards.

Those five sisters were all very fine seamstresses from Holland who had left their home country when they were all still very young and able to work with their hands. With all their earned money they had purchased that home in Velbert, Rhineland, Poststreet 56. They moved a level higher because of the outside upkeeping, and we moved to the first floor.

We children were considered everybody's girl and boy, "a maid for all things." We did a lot of running for them, which we did not mind as long as it did not cut into church work.

Mom had a lot of fun with these old ladies, and they were very good to us children. She did not believe in too many visitations; as the Bible says in Proverbs 25:17: "Don't visit your neighbor too often, or you will wear out your welcome."

Mom had my sister clean the street sidewalk one day. There were many people walking. My sister Inge had stopped to talk to someone she knew from school when Mom called out from the window, "Miss Inge, if you are done cleaning the street, you may go home." Inge was really very embarrassed because it sounded like she was a maid to a very rich family, as she told us later.

Washing Machines

The oldest of the sisters was in her eightieth year and very mentally disturbed. Her name was Elisabeth.

When these sisters had a disagreement, they asked Mom to be the judge. At times they came and complained about Marie, who was the youngest and often did not perform her duties or had forgotten something. So they would tell Mom to tell the "young kid" off, who was ten years older than Mom. They never became physical with each other, but were very loud at times.

Elisabeth had decided in her own mind to leave the home one spring day, so there was an emergency call made to the rescue department by the sisters that she had disappeared and needed to be found. Much talking and crying went on, so Mom went through the park, looking and searching for that oldest sister. Mother saw the green rescue van from far off and the men trying to coax Elisabeth into the van to no avail.

Mother had no difficulties. Elisabeth saw a familiar face and came to Mom right away. She got into the van and Mom was invited to get in also, but declined. She did not want to be seen being taken away in that notorious green van.

It was not too long after that episode when a very large truck parked outside our home. We were all very puzzled. From our window we were able to follow everything that was going on. These drivers were hauling out one washing machine after another. These were very high-class Konstructa washing machines. They unloaded twelve of them up and down our driveway.

No one apparently had ordered them, until Elisabeth mentioned having ordered all of them. Our cute old lady was able to convince a very large company that she was in need of all those washing machines.

Dad called the company and informed them about all these machines sitting in our driveway in all kinds of weather, and that a lady in the house who was mentally disturbed had made the order, so there would be no monetary reimbursement.

Late at night, the company had sent a large semi to pick all those machines up.

Teen Years

My parents placed me in a boarding school that was attached to a hospital. I continued my high school years away from my family, although every two weeks I spent my days off at home. It was about a three-hour train ride, and I needed my Mom's shoulder to cry on. I was only fifteen years old.

At boarding school, I did household chores and learned how to clean—to actually get on my knees to clean corners. One time I was told to clean doors "the right way" and I told my supervisor that doors need not be cleaned because the dirt could not cling on doors so slick and shiny. I learned a lesson! Doors are cleaned from the bottom up, so that no black streaks could drip down.

Even as a young girl, I had a notion that I was called for a nobler lifestyle. I was assigned to clean single rooms that were all occupied with first-class patients who received special treatment and who had their own private doctors.

There were fifteen rooms to clean before lunch, so I had to hurry. It was after lunch one day and I was called in the office and told I had forgotten to clean one of the rooms. I said, "It is time for me to go to lunch. I am done cleaning." As I walked to my room, I had a visitor tell me to pack my suitcase, that I was dismissed and I should go home.

Well, I threw myself on the bed, refused to leave, and cried my heart out. I could not visualize telling my mother I was fired from my job. I started to pack, my heart all in knots. What was I going to tell my parents? The train would leave in about one hour, so I needed to hurry. I was very much engulfed in my thoughts, so I didn't hear someone coming into my room. My supervisor came and told me I could stay.

It was much later, perhaps weeks or a month, when Mom asked me about the incident. I had not uttered one syllable about it, then she let me read a letter she received from my supervisor. She had known all along about my dilemma and she had not said a word. Thank you, Mom.

A New Job

Some good friends of my parents from church wanted to know if us two girls wanted a different job in a lab research center, and my sister and I both agreed. We surely would make more money and have weekends off. It was a good change, and we all were together as a family.

We paid Mom household money for room and board, and she filled our hope chest for future years. It was a joy looking through our chest with new towels and bed linens. Mom then started collecting sterling knives, forks, spoons, and larger sets of dinner plates for the time we would get married. She was so thoughtful.

We worked for about a year in that research center, then Mother lined up a job for my sister to work in a sewing place where she could gain knowledge in the manufacturing of garments. Even at a young age, Inge showed great interest, talent, and ability in sewing. This would become her bread and butter in later life.

Ella

There are three main kinds of businesses: working with people, money, or things.

Life inside walls with "things," smelly oils and paints, was not for me. I had to find my kind of business: working with people. I was soon to find out about my calling. I had a desire to become a missionary to foreign countries, but I only knew the German language and needed to learn English.

My aunt Elisabeth came to visit us one day and wanted my mother to trade places with her, to be a nursemaid to a distant relative who was mentally disturbed and also might be demon possessed, according to my aunt. We children and Dad were not too pleased with this idea.

Ella was an old school friend from Mom's earlier days. We all felt Mother was not strong enough to deal with her, maybe wrestling her to the ground or getting hurt, and she might be gone for a long time.

I was in my late teen years but not qualified to handle a job like that away from home, I thought. But something in me made room for adventure. Using my Bible as a guide, I read in Jeremiah 29:14, "I will bring you back again to your own land." That was good enough for me, and I told my family I was willing to go. I did not have too much opposition, nor any experience, but my adventurous spirit had gotten the best of me. This was my opportunity to get away from the work I did not care for.

I had never been around a person who was mentally ill. I had never seen a drunkard or unruly people. I was soon to find out. What gave me a great sense of security was that I could rely on my praying parents, brother, and sister. Ella taught me to open my ears and eyes to hurting people in this world, and I was on my way.

Ella was a lady of about forty years when she was placed in a Christian rehabilitation facility designed as a home-away-from-home for many mentally ill patients. It was located away from heavy city traffic, way up high in the hills and beautiful forest. I was going to spend some time with a lady I did not know and had only heard about.

Ella Decker, the same as my maiden name, only knew me by my first name. She was a slender lady with a dark complexion. When I saw her, she appeared very agitated and constantly on the move.

A second bed had been placed in the room, and the two windows were barred. Ella had to be watched twenty-four hours a day and I was her guard, locked in with her. I knew people were praying, but for me it was not enough. I was afraid and had no phone inside the room. The toilet was outside in the hallway, so every time I had to go, Ella had to come with me. The dining room was on the other side of the building, so it was an adventure to get out of the room.

Ella was an early riser. The very first morning, I felt her hands around my neck and closing in on my throat. My, did I jump out of bed in no time. Ella mumbled constantly, "My God, my God," stripped naked with hands stretched up high.

At times we ate breakfast very late because Ella would refuse to get dressed. She only wore black. Anything bright she would tear or throw in the garbage.

Quite often we had to eat in the room, with Ella half-dressed. Meals were brought to our room. Ella would not eat by herself, so I had to feed her the meals. However I tried to encourage her independence, although she would protest by pouring soup over me or on the floor. Fasting and praying were done for Ella around the clock.

Ella walked in her room, up and down with hands lifted up and mumbling, "Almighty God!" Her conversations didn't make any sense, although I understood only bits and pieces.

Ella was a widow and had promised her late husband to never get married again. A friend's wife had died not long after that, and Andrew had asked her to marry him, but she declined and became very depressed over it. She had no children and had moved in with her mother and became more depressed as the years went by.

Her mother was to get some Social Security for Ella, but she was told that she had to be of sound mind and able to write. Her mother was also a poor widow and needed some extra help.

Aunt Elisabeth, who knew Ella quite well, came with eyewitnesses to record her signature; one from the post office and a clerk from city hall, who was her daughter. We needed Ella to sign two documents.

After hours of coaxing, talking, and begging, Ella gave her signature to one of the documents, but we needed one more. With her hands lifted above her head, she pronounced her upcoming death by hanging. I would have liked to know her state of mind.

We had one more signing episode in front of us. The postal clerk who knew my aunt quite well told her to get the last signature any way she could and that he was leaving. Well, he was gone and we started to pray. We stormed heaven. We would not let Ella go to sleep until she had signed, and she must have known it because it was not very long before she lifted the pen and in no time she came through and gave us her last signature. Thank you, Ella.

One day, Ella had a very bad day and did not get dressed until noon. I put her underskirt on, but she took it off. So I started putting on socks, but she took them off. I finally got a book and tried to occupy my brain with something lovely, although it was difficult to put my mind on anything in a small room with a very dim light with someone chorusing around and always on the defensive.

I was hoping and praying that this soon would pass. Lord, when would my time be up? I had made a commitment and was going to stay with it. I was in seclusion with Ella and would stick it out, although only in my fifth week.

A letter from my dad was very hopeful. He was going to come and stay with me for a few days. Dad's room was next door, and it was very comforting to me just to know about his presence. He could not do very much, just pray.

Ella had become very quiet for a while, and I needed to be aware of an attack. Very quietly, she put her hands under my pillow, searching for the key. She became very aggressive because I would not let her get it and she was out to get me. I swung my legs over the bed and got into position to fight if she would attack me, but she stood there in front of me and said, "Christel, can you see the cross over the door?"

"No," I said. "Can you?"

She nodded and remarked, "I cannot hurt you. Around you is a fiery wall."

Thank you, Lord.

I just had my back turned away from her for a few moments, only to hang up a broom.

Well, I knew she could be quick, but to just disappear into nowhere was very puzzling to me. I had heard she was demon possessed, so she could have gone on a celestial trip, but that was not a good enough explanation to the police and rescue department. "Lord, help me find Ella," I prayed.

I had pushed the emergency alarm and people from everywhere in the resort came flying, trying to help, assist, and search. The home was combed from top to bottom, from the attic to the basement. Some had gone outside, looking behind trees, and even stopped cars. I did finally go back to the room to sort out the predicament I was in. There she was, standing by the window and sucking her thumb. She turned toward me as if nothing had happened.

"Ella," I said, "where have you been?" She just looked at me with her dark eyes, ready to claw me. I held my ground, not showing any fear, not backing off, making eye contact, and after about ten minutes she pointed toward the bed. She had crawled under my bed against the wall. Then I saw dust particles on her dress and I knew she had told me the truth.

I needed some time off and asked Aunt Elisabeth to take over for a few days. Easter was just days away and I wanted to go home. I went for about a week and was ready to come back when she called me and let me know that Ella had ran away. She had stopped a car and hitchhiked all the way home with a total stranger.

At home she went up to her room and jumped out of her window from the second floor of her home onto a pile of manure. The rescue crew assisted her and committed her to a mental institution.

I had come home on a visit from England when I visited her in the mental ward. She knew me and smiled. I asked her if she would write me a postcard, which she did and just signed it, "Ella."

England

My job with Ella was over and I thought, *Now what?* I felt time was running out. I recall one morning when I was alone in the house, making a plea before God that I was not getting off my knees until I heard from God in heaven and sending me to a mission field, and I meant it.

It was about noon that day when Mom came home and handed me an address from England. An elderly couple requested an au pair girl (nanny) who would work for pocket money in exchange for free room and board. The couple, Mr. and Mrs. Neil, were retired from the Commonwealth of England. They were long-time ambassadors to various countries, including Burma.

Mrs. Neil had multiple sclerosis, and at the age of seventy she was paralyzed almost up to her neck, although she was able to use some of her fingers for writing.

The Lord had answered my prayer! In three weeks I was in England. I boarded a plane from Duesseldorf to London, which was my first airplane ride.

Unable to speak one word of English made me aware of my dilemma, and not being able to talk or understand made me feel so alone. Mr. Neil and a chauffeur met me at the London airport. My first hurdle was immigration. I had my guitar and was asked through an interpreter if I had come to make money as an entertainer. Mr. Neil came to my aid and showed them the necessary papers, then I was free to go.

We traveled just north of London to a small community. The Neil's house was full of people who worked for them. There were two cooks who took turns, as well as a day nurse and a night nurse. Each staff member had a relief.

I served as Mrs. Neil's close companion, taking her out in a wheelchair and doing certain exercises with her. There was a full-time gardener and a substitute, a chauffeur, and a housekeeper. Mrs. Neil provided me with a tutor for the purpose of learning English, but after three sessions I dismissed him because he only spoke French and English. He was unable to explain certain words to me. For instance, the word "kind" means child in German but has a different meaning in English.

So I ventured out on my own because I didn't want to waste good money on a tutor who couldn't help me. Every new word I learned I wrote down in a little booklet, and I carried a dictionary day and night. And I listened to the radio to pick out what they were talking about.

Mrs. Neil's sister Netty came out every Thursday. Her title was Lady Braithwait and her husband was Lord Braithwait. Both ladies received intensive massages, so I was able to do things on my own. During my stay, I felt as though I was elevated to high society. Often, Rolls-Royces were parked in our drive yard.

Mr. and Mrs. Neil attended high functions in London. Often my wardrobe was not quite suitable, so the same ladies who came and dressed Mr. and Mrs. Neil also dressed me.

Mrs. Neil's brother, Noel Baker, invited us to his home in Kensington, London. He was the winner of the Nobel Prize for literature in 1959 for writing the book Arms Race. I was still having great difficulties with my reading abilities, so I did not read it.

It took me almost six months until I could understand some of the spoken language. I was thrilled when I was finally able to understand a story on the radio.

After several months I knew many words. Grammar and consolidating those words to make sentences became the more difficult task. Speaking correctly was going to be almost mandatory. Initially I was living in a silent world, not being able to talk or be understood. My first real language challenge lay ahead.

I used to wear high-heeled shoes, which were very fashionable at the time, and I developed a corn on one of my toes, so I needed some corn remover. I ventured out by myself to a pharmacy and tried to explain the pain on my toe. I explained that I needed something for my "chicken eye"—the direct translation for what in German is called *"ein Huehnerauge."* It was most complicated. Not to just one or two, but to three people I tried to explain what I needed. I finally bent my arms and crowed like a chicken—gawk, gawk, gawk—and pointed to my foot.

One of the clerks invited me to come behind the counter to look for remedies by myself. We had quite a time. I left with corn remover, a new word for my English vocabulary treasure.

Mr. and Mrs. Neil were very interesting people, and interesting people came to visit them, usually for high tea. The guests were seated in the drawing room. Mr. Neil was a real gentleman. Every time one of us entered the room, even the housekeeper who served the tea or myself, he would show us courtesy and stand up until I was seated or the housekeeper was done serving tea. He was well into his eighties at the time.

One day, one of the ladies asked me to fill her cup with tea and add a level teaspoon of sugar. It sounded to me like "eleven" teaspoons of sugar. So I started counting (in German) and thought, *Why doesn't she pour the tea in the sugar?* until she held my arm still and showed me by stretching her finger across the spoon to teach me about a level teaspoon of sugar.

It was always a long way to get to the bus. The busses ran every hour, and it was a forty-five minute walk across a field to get to the bus stop. The walk was not bad in summer, but in winter snowdrifts would make the field road much more difficult to walk. I even encountered whiteouts. From the bus, we would continue our route using the subway to London.

A tribe of gypsies settled halfway across the field, and those living in our small community were none too happy with their intrusion. When walking the road, all of us would make a large circle around them so as not to get too close because we were scared. The gypsies acted differently. They cooked outside and had many children who would roam around.

One day, I was on my own going across the field, avoiding getting close to the gypsies. I was concentrating on my bus schedule when I saw the bus in the distance. It came to a stop and then proceeded to leave. Now it would be another hour until the next bus! Oh, somehow I had miscalculated my bus schedule.

I was very disappointed about the delay when suddenly an old truck tried to pass me on the rocky road. The driver noticed I had just missed the bus and offered me a ride into Watford to the subway station, which I accepted. Later, I found out he was the Gypsy king of the tribe of whom we were all so afraid. Thereafter, I didn't make a circle around the gypsies anymore, because I had made friends.

With my limited knowledge of English, I had the audacity to put in for a nursing career opportunity at a nearby hospital in Watford, near Aldenham. I had all my school transcripts from Germany translated, from grade school (during the war years) up to my junior year and high school.

After one year of teaching myself the English language, I was accepted as a pre-nursing orderly from May 1959 to September 1959. I was then accepted into the program on probation because of my limited English.

The first three months were very intense: anatomy and physiology, bedside nursing care, chemistry with pharmacology combined, and the law of the land. All the nursing candidates were isolated in a boarding school where we could fully concentrate on our studies.

I had to get serious about study habits. Every week we had a quiz. I still remember one of my anatomy tests about the hip joint. The way I memorized it was the way I wrote it down. My brain was in high gear. During the day I studied anatomy, and during the night hours I studied the English language. My sleeping hours were cut dramatically. I had to learn how to take notes so I would be able to read them again. At time I felt my brain was at a saturation point, not able to take in any more foreign material. And I was not alone.

I could have benefited from prior studies in human anatomy in high school, but we were not taught in Germany like the girls in England, so I had to do double duty. After three months in confinement at nursing headquarters, we were ready to start our nursing career.

We received a different uniform: black shoes, black nylons, a large, starched white cap, a gray and white striped dress, a stiff white belt, and a white apron. Our outdoor uniform was a trench coat with a cap, black shoes, and black nylons. A long, dark blue cape with red on the inside was our coat for walking between buildings and when it was cold. I was very proud of my uniform.

The nurses shared rooms as junior, and later as seniors we had single rooms. A housekeeper attended to our rooms and collected our daily laundry. On our days off, we had breakfast in bed if we wished, and that I did. We worked hard on the wards, which had forty beds.

One night, four of us nurses decided to reward ourselves with an evening out at a Chinese restaurant. This was one eatery where you never came away hungry. We had just finished eating when the owner came out and greeted us. He recognized me from when he was a patient on one of the wards where I worked.

Nurses in outdoor uniforms were easily recognizable. We were given ten percent off all purchases in stores and various restaurants. It was also mandatory for nurses in uniform to assist in any emergencies on the roads or whenever a need would arise.

The waiter handed us our ticket just before the owner invited us to come with him upstairs. Not knowing we had eaten, he seated us around the table and offered us another menu, which we accepted. We ate again—the second time in less than an hour. I could not bring myself to tell him about our previous dinner. We almost had to call an ambulance for ourselves. Some big-bellied nurses walked out of that restaurant that night!

Tea is England's main beverage, next to—I think—beer.

The women's surgical ward was most interesting. I was most fascinated by the diversity of young and old, very sick and not so sick, Jamaican ladies and ladies from India, Scotland, and Ireland. Everyone got along very well. There was no fighting or calling people names. Forty females and all in harmony!

My shift was between 8 P.M. to 8:00 A.M. Two nurses were assigned to a ward, always a senior nurse and a junior nurse. The nights seemed to resemble days. Late at night, patients from the operating room required close observation. Nurses would do vitals every fifteen minutes, watching blood infusions or ringer lactate. Certain surgeries were done on certain days, so we had some nights that were easier than others.

It was required of any senior nurse after the third night to know a patient's name and diagnosis, the medication they were on, and the day of their admission.

Making my rounds every so often, following moans and groans, I would often hear, "Nurse, may I have a cup of tea?" I would say, "Yes, but tell no one." Then from the other side of the ward I heard a similar request—"A cup of sha (English tea), please." Sometimes I ended up making ten to fifteen cups of tea for the patients. Every morning at about 4 A.M., we made porridge for the whole ward for the day's breakfast. I started to enjoy tea, learning the secret of good-tasting tea was never to wash the teakettle, and when pouring the tea, always put cream in the cup first.

Midterm Nursing Exam

Midterm exams were at hand. Anatomy, my most exciting subject, was also my weakest. If only I would pass the anatomy and physiology exam, I would be in the driver's seat.

I studied almost day and night, memorizing what I could. This was the time I prayed so sincerely, "Oh, please Lord, let the rapture be tonight. Come now. What have I gotten myself into?" All kinds of thoughts penetrated my mind: *Why don't you just go home?* or *Just don't take the test.* But I knew I had made a commitment to follow through.

There was never any money for extras. My money was needed for buying texts and study books. Tithing and giving offerings became secondary. The Bible had been my guide and I knew that giving was part of worship. "But Lord, my wallet is empty," was my cry. "What do you want me to do?"

My friend, nurse Elaine Bunkert, was a Seventh Day Adventist engaged to one of the doctors, a dermatologist. Elaine invited me to her fiancée's house one Sunday. In my heart the Lord and I made a promise that if He would supply me with nursing books, I would tithe. It was not the right way to do it, but the Lord heard my plea and knew my heart.

After dinner, an older gentleman took me in the library to look at some books. They were mostly medical books, with some travel and law books. I looked at some of the collection when he turned to me and said, "If you see any books you like, you can take them." I walked off with three books about internal medicine, surgeries, and bedside nursing. I felt so rich. Those books were way above my head because they were doctor's handbooks, but the Lord came through and I honored Him with my offerings.

Elaine's fiancée was a lecturer in one of our classes and he mentioned to Elaine about me having a doctor's handbook. Her fiancée wanted to know if I was pursuing the medical field to become a doctor.

We all had to go to the London Hospital to take our practical and written exams. The waiting period was very difficult on all of us. Our grades were displayed publicly, and I had great joy when I saw I had passed everything except tropical diseases. This was a subject I now would concentrate on for the next three months. With that one exception, I passed with flying colors.

We received a different cap. Our belt was now dark blue and our dress a light blue. We were all very proud. Now we had more responsibilities on the wards. We were left in charge and received the key for the drug cupboard.

The nurses had to take turns on the wards for tuberculosis and tropical diseases. After nine months, we were all pulled from the wards and went back to school for another four weeks. The study load was getting increasingly more intense. There was no time to play—not for me.

Basic nursing became more sophisticated. Pharmacy, knowing about drugs, and nursing law were very high on the list. First there was anatomy, then the study of diseases, surgical procedures, tests and lab work, drawing blood, doing infusions, and giving shots.

The burn unit was the most difficult place for me to work. Once, just as I had come back from my two-hour time off, I was sent with a child who was severely burned to another hospital that dealt with burn victims who needed skin grafts. An ambulance drove us at high speed to a London hospital for further treatment. It is always difficult when a child is in distress and too young to understand.

Another incident I recall involved an older woman who needed blood and was very nervous as she came in. As we were getting her ready, she grabbed my arm in desperation and pulled me close to her, saying, "Nurse, I am unable to drink that much blood." With great assurance I helped her to understand the procedure and she became peaceful.

In our geriatric unit, one of the student nurses was told to give certain patients a glass with mouthwash at night to place their dentures in. Instead of giving the patient a glass, she went around and collected all the dentures from the patients in one bowl. Oh my, what a mess for the nightshift who discovered all the teeth in a large container!

Squashed

Visiting hours were twice daily—once in the afternoon and the other time from 7:30 to 8:30 P.M. every evening. Everyone helped to get the patients ready. Right after the evening meal we had to rush to get forty patients comfortable and presentable for their loved ones.

During visiting time, two nurses stayed behind if we had some very sick patients, while the others went for their meals. We allowed two visitors at the bedside because it was very stressful for some of the patients.

We were ready. We had our big double doors opened when I noticed at 7:45 P.M. that the visitors from downstairs were still waiting. I informed my nurse quickly and ran down to find out why the doors were not open. I called my German nurse friend and I heard a whimpering from a far corner. I had noticed something very funny at first. I started pulling the curtain around that bed let in the visitors who had been cheated by almost twenty minutes of visiting time, then discovered my friend was squashed under a very obese woman who had rolled off the bedpan while my friend Wally tried to help her get off.

I tried to get my friend from under that woman, with much difficulty. We notified the switchboard to send us two hefty men to get the woman back into her bed.

Both Wally and the patient had bruises; nothing too serious, but a lot of paperwork.

Nursing at Nighttime

We always made the best of every shift, nighttime or daytime. It seemed we had more time off at night; long hours, but more days off. I just made the best of every situation.

On nights we had an hour lunch break and some of us went for walks. Sometimes I studied or took a nap.

Walking on a hot summer night was a delight. But on that particular night, we were with six nurses when a patrol car came by and offered us a ride through town. We knew some of the officers and we were all in our uniforms, so we had nothing to fear. But we were very late, having extended well over our lunch break. We all tried to get back to our posts but were caught. Our supervisor, Miss Ham, called us one at a time into her office to give us a fair warning. I was told she had not expected it from me to climb into a patrol car and do some cruising with officers on call.

I had a couple of days off and returned to my men's medical ward. It was always very important to me to get a good and thorough shift exchange report when I was in charge.

I had a new girl, a first-year nursing student from Korea, who was very apprehensive and frightened. She begged me not to stay away too long for my lunch. We had two people who were very sick and dying and were in side rooms with special lights on.

Working on a men's ward with forty patients, all having breathing difficulties, I thought was a very frightening experience for me when I first started night shift. I was sure they were all dying. I had not heard so many men all breathe together and snoring in one place. It took me a while to learn and get used to a symphony made by sleeping men.

I had promised nurse Mimi to just get my dinner and be right back, which was about ten minutes. When I came back, all the big lights in the wards had been turned on and every person on that ward was awake at about 1 A.M. However eventually nurse Mimi did get used to the night shift, and I enjoyed working with her.

Big Eddy

Psychiatric, or hypnotic medicine, deals with the study, investigation, and treatment of mental disorders, and a great deal of progress has been made in treatment.

Nurse Hall (Pat) and I were second-year students and had just finished three months in the operating room when we were assigned to the psychiatric ward.

It took a lot of getting used to working with adults who were totally lost within themselves. We were experiencing firsthand shock treatment, insulin shock treatment, and patients who were totally out of control.

Two nurses were assigned to always accompany each other. We were never to be alone under any circumstances. Our duty was to observe and write down our experiences.

Eddy was a big, black man who was diagnosed as manic-depressive. He wanted to marry me and searched me out as soon as I came on duty, then followed me around and would not leave me alone. I told him I only had a few weeks on the ward and would soon leave, but that was not enough.

It was around noon one day and it seemed the ward was almost empty. I was not thinking about my partner when the door opened and an aide called Eddy for lunch. But Eddy just said, "No lunch for me." The door closed and I heard the key turn on the other side. It suddenly occurred to me I was alone with Big Eddy. I pounded on the door and called for someone to let me out, then rattled windows and banged on the wall. Eddy started to help me bang and knock and yell. Suddenly he turned to me and asked, "Miss Decker, why don't you use your key?" He pointed to my apron pocket. Here I had a key in my pocket the whole time, and Eddy had to remind me. He had a much better understanding at that moment than I.

A party was planned for all the student nurses and the patients we had observed who were able to attend. Dinner was prepared, with dancing afterward. Eddy asked me to dance with him but I told him I could not dance. I was going to be late for that event. I wanted to miss dinner and the dance, but when I came near the dining room, Eddy spotted me and had a chair reserved next to him. I sat down. The music started and I wanted to disappear. John, an ex-policeman who had tried to commit suicide with carbon monoxide and had the most violent behavior, pulled me out of my chair and onto the middle of the dance floor. Well, I hobbled with him just to please him, then Eddy stood up and pulled me away from John. A shout was heard, the music stopped, and Eddy and I were the only ones doing the jig in the middle of the dance floor. I never did learn how to dance.

After my time on the psychiatric ward, I worked with orthopedic patients with mostly broken bones from the clavicle to complicated arm and leg fractures, hip fractures, and knee injuries.

In the late fifties and early sixties, patients were placed in body casts, plaster jackets, and large contraptions with pins through large bones, steadied with heavy weights. Nursing care was to prevent bedsores. Many patients were fed and ate in a prone position, lying flat on a hard bed. Patients stayed for many weeks, often six weeks or longer, until healing had taken place.

Most orthopedic patients were quite well, their health good, and often they were young adults. I remember a twenty-year-old named Bob who was in a traction splint. He had a pin through his tibia, the bone under his knee, with weights to maintain the alignment of his bones. Bob could only pull himself up by using a pulley. This ward had forty patients in one room, usually all bored with nothing to do and just waiting to go home. So of course, it was one of the noisiest wards. There was never a dull moment.

Frequently we pushed beds together when patients wanted to play cards or other games. Bob always enjoyed when others received painful treatments such as injections, having blood drawn, or an infusion. You could hear him yell across the ward and let others know how he enjoyed their pain. This was a daily occurrence.

One day when it was my turn to give all the antibiotics (usually as injections) and with other nurses in agreement, I searched out the largest syringe with a very long needle and a red liquid. Bob started his yells again to let the others know how he enjoyed their pain. When we had a procedure to perform, we would normally draw the bed curtains. However, when it was Bob's turn, we left the curtains open and just told him to turn around. Bob took one look at the syringe and needle and turned white. He was cured and never again uttered any more of those joyful, teasing yells.

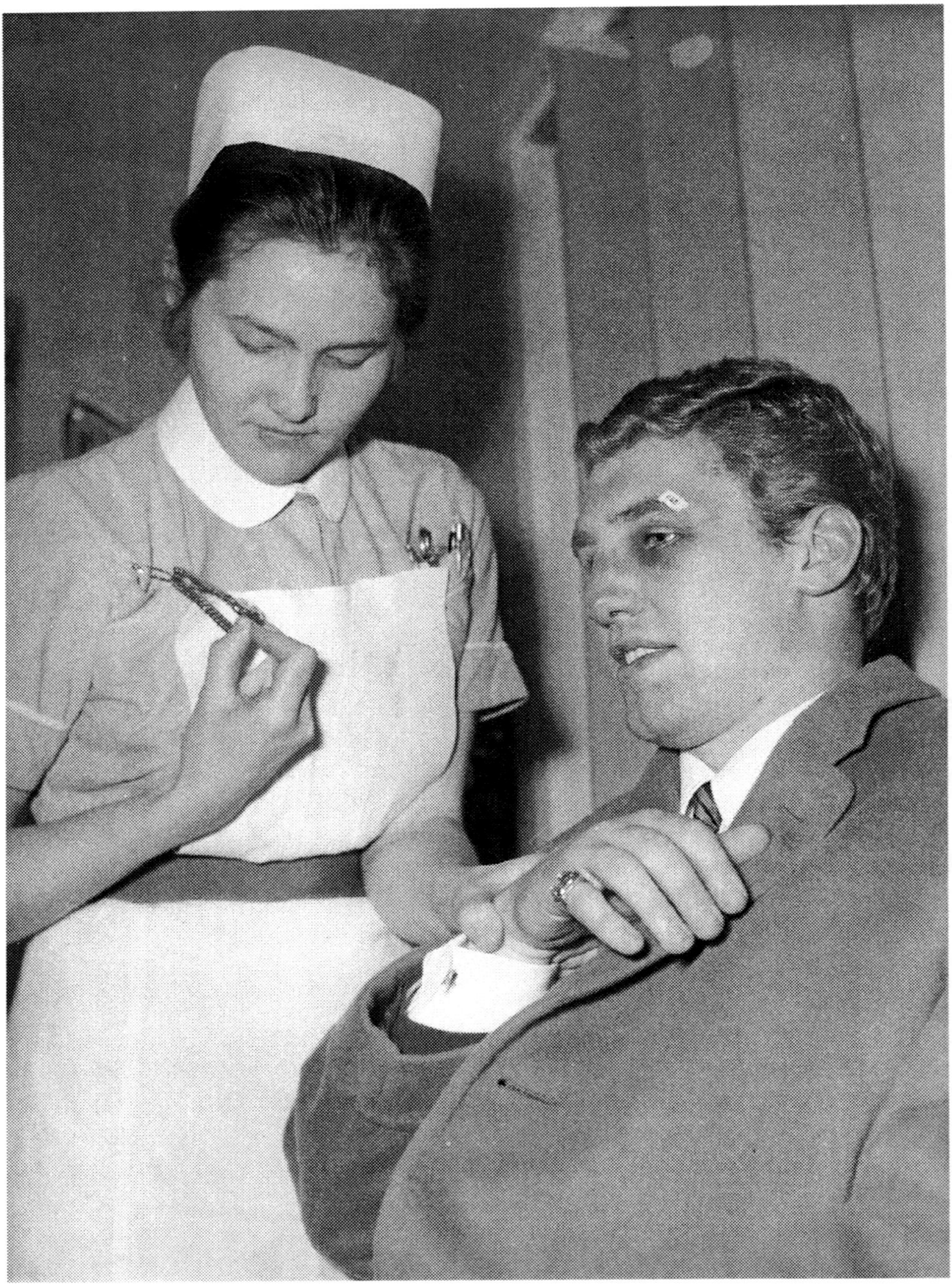

Emergency Room

It was my turn to start in the emergency room. I was in my second year and enjoyed the change. This was a very hectic place. Sirens, ambulances, people coming and going, nurses rushing from one place to another. Moaning and groaning was heard all over.

My job in the beginning was to have treatment trays ready, clean and sterilize instruments, admit patients, and take care of relatives until I had a routine and knew what I was doing. If it was hectic, questions had to wait until later.

I recall an incident that took place one day during lunchtime. The crowd had been taken care of. Some people were still lingering, waiting for a ride home or for reports. It was unusually quiet, so I was left in charge. Others had gone for lunch, some went off duty. There was always a lot of cleaning up, preparing new trays for treatments.

Anything could happen at any time of the day. I was aware of an ambulance just arriving outside, but was surprised when a crew of news people was coming in with the patient. I quickly assessed the situation. On a stretcher was a very famous boxer, Bill Walker. He had been boxing the night before, and on his way home had a near fatal car accident with his Jaguar sports car on the M1 freeway from London. He was ejected from his car, landed, and rolled down an embankment. He had a wound near his eye that needed stitches. As I was taking care of him, cameras were flashing. I had to pose. Billy smiled at the crew as he was wheeled into the side room for further evaluation and treatment.

The next day, there I was on the front page of the *London Daily Mirror* with a smiling boxer. A young boy came in for treatment the next day and only wanted to be treated by the nurse who treated Billy Walker.

All About Moms and Babies

The maternity ward was a very healthy and exciting place to work, but I spent most of my time on a gynecology ward, which was a place where patients were hurting, suffering, and wanting babies but unable to conceive. A lot of research was going on. Very painful and difficult procedures were performed. A mixed group of patients were side by side; some mothers who were on total bed rest because of internal bleeding, others having twins and needing rest; miscarriages, or self-induced abortions. We as nurses were not to show any emotions, but nurses have feelings and can hurt just as much as anyone. My motto was always to bring cheer to the patients and never lose the personal human touch.

Friendship

Friendship among the nurses was important. We could only be friends who were in the same class and also could share a room with them or going shopping. To speak to a senior nurse, we had to wait until we were spoken to, unless it was about a patient's welfare. A junior nurse could never start a conversation during dinnertime or in a hallway or while on coffee break. Nurses were called in the office if they did not abide by that rule.

Men's Medical

It was after midnight. I had two patients dying and was very much concerned. I stayed with them as much and as long as I could. A third nurse was requested because of the workload. The older man had died right after midnight. We had special advice what to do in the first hour.

If he was Jewish, we were not to touch him because we were unclean. On one of the occasions, we did not know him and prepared for pickup first thing in the morning.

Our supervisor just came by to check on the chart and yelled, "He is Jewish!" So, what to do? We had all gotten hold of him and tried to put on his pajamas, but he had been dead for a couple of hours and so he was not limber anymore. We wanted him to look very normal in bed so the rabbi would not notice our mistake. We later heard he had to perform special duties to make the body clean.

My second patient had died, so Nurse Chapman and I had to do the usual tasks. We were just trying to put his gown on when the apparently dead body sat up and sneezed and laid down again. We both yelled. The hair on my neck stood up. We almost lost our composure.

We had learned that there was a nervous reaction—the man was dead, but not quite. Well, he was pronounced dead the second time.

I had just returned from a long weekend and started my nightshift. I insisted on a good shift exchange after a weekend separation. Making my rounds, seeing old and new patients, was very informative for me. As I came to Mr. Smith, he was most eager to see me and told me about his experience while I was gone.

Sometimes a relief nurse is at a disadvantage because she would be there one night and on another ward the next night. I had learned that Mr. Smith, who had a hernia operation, had difficulties breathing and did not feel too good.

I made sure to keep a very close eye on him. Every hour I made my rounds and noticed that Mr. Smith was awake and gasping for air. I connected the oxygen tank and supplied him with fresh air, then called for help. In no time, the emergency team arrived. I had to leave then and attended to my other patients.

The next night when I came on duty, I was informed that Mr. Smith had been moved to the cardiac department. For me that was the end of it. I went to visit him when I was relieved from the night shift, and he told me I had saved his life.

Many weeks later, we were serving dinner and someone had called for me, so I stepped away from the dinner cart. Here came Mr. Smith with one hand behind his back. He came toward me and gave me a kiss on the cheek, handed me a large box of chocolates, and walked away.

Twenty-four Roses

Night shift was always very strenuous. I managed to get five days off in row, from Friday through Saturday, for one week. The following week I was due three days—Sunday, Monday, and Tuesday—then back on duty Wednesday night. It was Easter. My friend, Jerry, had taken me to the London Airport on Good Friday right after my nightshift. By eleven o'clock that morning I was at the Duesseldorf Airport, where Dad and Mom picked me up.

When I left home, Mom told me to always have enough money to get home, enough for a one-way ticket. Days off went every quickly. Mom told me about a young man from church who was a missionary intern and had come to them asking for my hand in marriage, just to find out how I would react if they would tell me. G was a candidate for the mission in India. He also knew I was interested in missions and wanted to know more about me. We saw little of each other during the Easter weekend. We both kept it very secret, and with a secret love in my heart I went back to England. We did write some, but not as often as we should have. I did more praying. Concentrating on work, exams, tests, and being in love made the time go fast.

It was a very hot day in August. My birthday almost went unnoticed except for cards and letters from home when I saw the most beautiful bouquet of twenty-four (I counted them) long-stemmed red roses and a card from G, with his love. Someone across the English Channel was in love with me! It seemed the doors were wide open now and nothing could stop me and I would see the world. Africa was on my heart, but India, China, America, the Seven Seas, or even Australia all lay ahead of me, within my grasp. I was exuberant! Now I was going to finish my nursing, get my degree, and then out into the world. Those were my plans.

Our nursing finals were in the fall of 1962. Studying was of the utmost importance for me. I needed to pass my nursing exam. Again, we were all taken to the London Hospital. For two days we were tested on nursing skills, first aid, CPR, how to make beds, hold bandages, make splints, give shots, set trays with instruments for certain procedures, and assist doing lumbar punctures.

Oral tests were done then all the written exams (hospital and state board). A whole week was set aside for testing. After exams were over we had to wait six long weeks until all the results were in.

I wanted to get my master's degree and then go on to become a nursing instructor. But something different was in the wind. Just before Christmas, all the results were posted on the bulletin for everyone to see. I had passed all of the exams and had my new title: Miss Christel Decker, R.N.

England/Germany

England was dear to my heart. In my heart, though, I knew the time to leave England was at hand.

My R.N. certificate was in my pocket. I knew I could work almost anywhere I chose. At times I wondered if I was not making too hasty a decision. It was a most difficult time giving my resignation. I questioned whether I was doing the right thing.

On the other hand, I wanted to be a missionary. The whole world seemed to lie at my feet: Africa, India, Australia, and North America. I needed some time off, so my time at home in Germany was very relaxing, going to church, seeing all my friends, and nurturing my secret love.

G's internship made it very difficult for us to meet openly. It was very stressful for both of us to meet in church and not make it obvious, so we saw each other more from the distance than from close up. We called each other on the phone and went for walks after dark. This went on for a few months.

G was called before the mission board when he told all of them about me and our plans to go to India. I received a phone call from him the next day and was asked to meet him in the park nearby. I knew from his voice that something was up. We met in the park, and right away he said, "Christel, I cannot see you anymore. I was supposed to only talk to you on the phone, but I didn't think that it was right." He went on to tell me that if he married me, he could not go to India. I was devastated and puzzled. We broke up because I didn't want to stand in the way of him going to India.

G left the church, married his old girlfriend from his hometown, and later got a divorce. I learned later that someone in India was to be his future bride, if he would get there.

In the meantime, I had plans of my own. I wanted to go to Africa and I planned to sign a contract with the Royal College of Nurses in England for a two- to three-year commitment as a nurse in Durban, South Africa. My visa was in process and I had ordered all my uniforms. Just before it was time to go, however, a dear friend of my parents, who was also the principal of the German Bible School at that time, counseled me. He told me straight out that I was "on the run" like Jonah, the prophet. I didn't want to admit it, but

I knew he was right. Once again, I shifted gears and started to work in a Deaconess Hospital just up the road from where I lived. I saved my money for future plans. I only needed some money for housing and lodging, so after two years I enrolled in the German Bible School, Beroa.

Kranken-Schwester/Velbert

I had taken a sabbatical and moved in with my family in Velbert, Rheinland. It was so wonderful to stay home with Mom and Dad. My sister was married and lived close by. My brother was getting ready to attend the Bible school in Erzhausen, near Frankfurt. He wanted to study the Bible and become a minister for the Lord.

It was in the fall of 1963 when we all got into our car to take Guenter to the Bible school. This was a new chapter for our whole family. In a way, he made a way for me to become a student as well in later years.

The hospital in my hometown was five minutes away from our home. A quick trip through our garden and I was on the hospital lawn. I applied at the hospital and was accepted right away. I was allowed to wear my own uniform from England, which I felt much more comfortable in.

I started on the men's surgical ward with only four in one room. The limit allowed in a room was six patients. The workload was different from what I was used to, but I adjusted quite quickly.

Deaconesses, who are in my mind Protestant nuns, ran the hospital. They came from different convents, motherhouses as they were called. These nurses were always right, and I had to do a little fighting of my own. Some deaconesses were hiding behind their nun garb, covering up very little nursing education but well protected by their motherhouse.

I enjoyed nursing. Seeing patients come into the hospital very sick and then leave healthy—oh, what a blessing!

I liked the nightshift, but this shift meant I rarely saw the sun. Our hours were so long and exhausting. I slept the day away after these long shifts. My Dad also had a partial nightshift. He left around 5 P.M. and came home around 4 A.M. I went to work at 8 P.M. and came home at 8 A.M. My poor mother decided to work a nightshift schedule as well. That way, we all slept during the day.

In Germany, neighbors kept a close eye out for each other. As a result, our neighbors often wondered about our sleeping habits. To fool them, Mother did the laundry in the washing machine in the evening, hanging out the clothes on the clothesline to make the neighbors think she had done the wash first thing in the morning.

Often my dad and mom got me up in the afternoon to go for a ride in the country. I really enjoyed being pampered. Those were good old days — thanks for a wonderful memory.

Beroa Bible School

The Beroa Bible School, located near Frankfurt am Main, Germany, served as my hiding place or escape from my hurting heart. G, my ex-boyfriend, had just graduated from there. I needed time for healing, but the school reminded me of him.

Getting to know other students and making new friendships eased my pain eventually. I realized that I was not alone. Missions, far away places, the seven seas were now some of the things I thought about.

I knew English. Studying the Bible and learning about foreign countries were now my necessary prerequisites and priorities, I thought. Often during my quiet times, I wondered how my life would unfold. Once a week we had a fasting and prayer day. We were taught to get away by ourselves to seek God's guidance and learn to be quiet.

It was early in December, 1965. A day of fasting was set and a twenty-four hour session of prayer. We all had certain times to pray, usually two-by-two in the chapel for fifteen minutes to half an hour. The chapel was connected to the main building by a very long hallway, sparsely lit by a few small electric light bulbs. Frieda, my roommate, and I signed up for midnight to pray for half an hour. We agreed to wake each other up.

Our turn came. We were still very sleepy, so we snuggled into our robes and slippers and headed down three flights of stairs, passing the laundry room, the kitchen, the pantry, and the dining room on our way. Just as we arrived at the main stairs that led to the classrooms, two large figures in white, free-flowing garments came flying down the stairs, running in front of us toward the chapel. Frieda and I let out the biggest yell and scream. We clung to each other, not knowing what to expect. The chapel was still quite a distance away from us. The ghosts turned and passed us again and flew upstairs!

In the meantime, a bunch of girls had come to find out why we had screamed. Frieda and I almost lost our minds. We were on the way to pray— why did we have a ghostly visitation? With our yelling, we had awakened almost everyone. We were escorted to our rooms. One of the girls had read in the book of Esther that all would be killed: "Hamman sought to destroy all the Jews in the twelfth month, which was December." That is the month of Adar in the Jewish calendar. We thought we were all doomed. Fear was everywhere. All the girls crawled into one bed and comforted each other.

The night was over for us. We had seen ghosts and we needed to find out more about it. When morning came, Frieda and I had both lost our voices from screaming.

When we entered the dining room that morning, we were greeted by two male students who had been called into the office and told to apologize to us. We learned that they had planned to scare us on the way to the chapel. Well, it worked! The thought came to them when a change of fresh bed linen was delivered. Fear had entered my mind, however, and I had a hard time shaking it. Weeks, then months, went by and I could not walk through dark places. I needed deliverance.

Finally, spring came. Special meetings were planned for the students. Special speakers were lined up and I went forward to be prayed over. I was set free—it was almost instant. Praise the Lord!

Greener Pasture

As I was pulling away from home, searching for a greener pasture and more open space, Mom became sicklier but would not let us know. She had gained quite a lot of weight, which was an effect of starvation during the time of war, then her metabolism became out of control. Diabetes had set in, and insulin was on her daily menu.

Her whole body ached. It seemed it was on strike. Doctors and my mother were not a good combination. She dreaded going to them.

In her younger years there was a lot of insurance money involved and she needed a physical. The doctor had left the room for Mom to get into a hospital gown, but when he came back she had not moved and the doctor wondered if he had not made it clear to her what to do. She looked at him and said, "Doctor, what you want to feel, you feel through my clothes."

Now going to a doctor or seeing one was on her regular schedule. My poor Mom—she had learned how to overcome those obstacles.

In Alaska, in much later years, I had learned that Mom was in the hospital for breast surgery. It was no small trip to fly home, so I had ordered a dozen red roses via ham radio while above the Arctic, and as she told me later in a letter she was just on the way to her room from surgery when these roses arrived. She had not quite recovered, but she heard, "Frau Decker, roses from Alaska," and as Mom said, "In my stupor I hugged those roses, thorns and all."

Weeks later, Mom was still in the hospital and I had flown out to Anchorage for R&R. I enjoyed a little shopping and saw the most beautiful red, see-through nightgown and a matching color satin robe, which I purchased and airmailed to her home. My sister received the package and opened it, only to be outraged at me sending such sinful lingerie to her elderly mother. She drove to the hospital, having it in mind for Mom only to look at this nightgown set and for her to say, "I cannot wear this!" However, Mom unfolded it and her eyes became brilliant and very lustrous, and with a shout she explained, "I have been praying for a new nightgown!" She wore it with much pride.

Internship in Hamburg

After one year of biblical instruction, my way led me to Hamburg, a city by the Elbe River near the North Sea, a few hundred miles away from the Atlantic Ocean.

Pastor Rabe requested me because of my nursing education and because I was knowledgeable in the English language. I was to do district nursing combined with spreading the Good News.

The Elim church was the "mother church," serving many smaller, outlying churches, some located more than fifty miles away. Elim was a Pentecostal church, one of the largest Assembly of God churches in Germany. I was excited to stay in Hamburg, a city that does not sleep. The city has the largest inland harbor in Germany. Big ocean ships traveled the river's waterways into the city. A large tunnel was built under the river Elbe for trains, cars, streetcars, and a walkway for passengers. I walked it.

I was part of a large staff. There were four pastors-in-training, office staff, and two interns like me, as well as kitchen and cleaning personnel. Pastor Rabe was the senior pastor, and Siegfried served as our assistant pastor.

Hamburg Church Privacy

Privacy was a precious commodity. It seemed all the church members owned us. When no organ or piano player was available, I filled in to provide music in whatever service it was needed.

Pastor Rabe used his authority to get things done, and we did not even think to disagree. When I was asked to play, I only agreed under the condition that I would play the songs I knew. Quite often I used my guitar in smaller meetings. I was able to play the organ or piano when the songs were written in the keys of C, F, E, and A—all in flat. My time to practice was in the meetings with the senior citizens, who were quite tolerant and happy with me.

Everyone addressed staff by their first names, but we had to address the pastoral staff and members by their last name, or Brother or Sister, in a very formal way. None of the staff were teenagers so I requested a staff meeting to address the issue about addressing us in the proper way. We proposed either talking to us in a formal manner or dropping the formalities altogether for everyone.

The "old school" still thought "the children" should address their elders with "Missus" and "Mister," thus not using first names, which was more common in the USA.

The meeting was held and we all "toasted" with coffee and agreed to use the informal way to address each other. We dropped the "thee" and used the "thou" (*sie* and *du* in German).

Hamburg Church Activities

We two ladies did full-time visitation. We had about nine hundred members attending the Elim church in the Bachstr. To get to the outstations we used trains, busses, and subways. I got to know most of our members.

Next to visitations, we taught Sunday school and attended the youth choir with stringed instruments. There was also street evangelism—going from door to door. We were taking part in the senior club, making coffee, serving cakes, and giving biblical instruction. I did the singing part.

Summers were very hectic for us, taking control, having kid's crusades, and vacation Bible school. Every so often there were outings planned for young people, some in the mountains or near the ocean.

Our pastor was not in favor of having ladies wear long pants, short hair, or using any makeup, especially the ladies on his staff. In freezing weather we girls sneaked out of the church at 10 P.M. to go sledding. We wore long pants for our own protection, but this sneaking around was not to my liking.

I had received a French horn as a present and started to practice right away. The seniors in our church were always appreciative when I played a tune. Our brass band had about twenty-five members. It was not long before I was able to play the first Christmas song on my horn. I played piano or organ for my own enjoyment only, playing the guitar more frequently for others.

During the midweek services, when no official player was available, they asked me to do the honor and play an instrument to keep the folks in tune. I played the piano under one condition: that I could choose my own songs. I must be very honest and say that I did a lot of practicing at the old folks' home and at the senior club at our church.

One day I was asked to play for a funeral. An old lady from our church had died. Our pastor was in charge and requested me to play the organ in the funeral chapel. My very first impulse was to say, "No, way!" Well, our pastor had a way with us that we did not dare to go against his wishes. I practiced and practiced the songs I had chosen every day on our church organ.

"Lord," I prayed, "please keep me calm and collected. Sooth my nerves." I had no way to practice on the organ in the chapel, which was much too big for my liking but I entered the chapel and found the organ, although I felt scared.

The mourners were already gathering, and I played my preludes and the songs with the mourning family. Everything went quite well. As the casket was carried out, I played a medley and as I was looking for the button to lower the volume, I hit the wrong one and hit the keys full blast. It seemed the organ was running away with me. The casket could have easily opened because of that sudden volume from the keyboard. I fumbled and searched in the dark for that knob to lower the noise, feeling all alone in that dilemma. I needed to get out for fresh air.

Well, many church people spread the news. I was offered to have a professional tutor teach me playing the organ, but I refused because I had not planned to stay in that church for very long.

It was less than a year later when I resigned, and our Pastor Rabe died one month later.

Sister Crousart

A young married sister in the Lord, a fine Christian, lay dying in the hospital. For two weeks I spent every night with her. She died on a Sunday about 5 A.M.

The Hamburg Church was in full swing with revival meetings performed in a very large tent not far from the church. All the services went well. We had different speakers for weeks at a time. They were all housed in the church and we served all their meals and snacks, often until late at night.

The staff was all involved in meeting with new converts and follow-up. I had just come home from my nightly duty, staying awake all night with the dying sister. My aim was bed—I wanted to sleep for a week. The building was very noisy with guests coming and going. I even felt guilty sleeping during the day while other folks were working very hard.

I was in a deep sleep when a very noisy knock on the door awoke me. A staffer asked me if I could come and serve coffee and cake to the workers in the tent. I felt a little refreshed, so I agreed to help. I got ready, brewed coffee, and cut the cake to take across the parking lot to serve the workers. It was about a ten-minute walk.

On my way over, carrying a dinner tray with all the goodies and cups and spoons, I tripped over something and thought I had stepped on an electric cable wire. I made a complete turn and spun around, still holding onto my tray. Looking down I saw nothing lying on the ground, so I kept walking toward the tent. I experienced another of the same episode inside the tent.

Later on that night I was handed a note asking me to conduct a kid's crusade on Tuesday in another town. I packed my overnight bag, studied my material, and traveled on Monday by train to that distant place.

My assigned sleeping quarters were with an elderly widow lady. I arrived late that evening and she asked me what time she should set the alarm clock for or should she just wake me up? A meeting had been scheduled for me at the church at 10 A.M., so I needed to get going by 9 A.M. At 11 A.M., there was no movement in my room, so the sister came in and said, "It is already 11 A.M." Well, I had overslept! I jumped out of bed only to collapse right back into bed. I was unable to stand up. The whole room spun around me, and I was sick to my stomach.

This dear sister escorted me to the bathroom or anywhere I needed to go. Someone else had to take over the kid's crusade. In the back of the revival tent was an army cot, and there my very ill body stayed until I had a ride back home. The doctor from across the street visited me at home and prescribed bedrest for me for one week. His diagnosis: physical exhaustion. I was unable to do anything. Sitting up in bed, getting up to eat and going to the bathroom alone, were all out of the question. I needed around-the-clock care, which I got from all of my dear friends and co-workers. When I was lying down, I felt good. As soon as I lifted my head just a little, it felt like being on the high sea. My head would just spin round and round. My parents were notified, so prayer went up to heaven day and night and slowly but surely strength came back into my body.

The Psalms are so comforting. Psalm 42: "As the deer panted for the water…." Psalm 23: "Though I walk through the dark, lonesome valley…." Psalm 91:11: "He shall give His angels charge over thee."

For the next few weeks I needed to hang on to guardrails in order to steady myself, but my equilibrium slowly returned. This was the time of searching the scriptures. Jesus was my solid rock. A solid object was much appreciated at that time. There were times when my body and soul were fastened to a lasso and swung around. Praise Jesus for His love and assurance in time of trouble.

Thinking of Leaving

A dear old sister of the church, "Grandma," who was unable to go to church, received frequent visits from our staff. We were all assisting somehow. I usually helped out with shopping, bathing, taking care of her feet, and taking her for walks.

One day we were talking about far away places and I mentioned the Pentecostal World Convention in Rio de Janeiro, South America. It was the year 1967. It would have been an unthinkable dream for me to visit.

Traveling has been my hobby. I had visited places in Europe like England, Norway, Denmark, Austria, Belgium, and Holland. But I dreamed of faraway places. Oh, to see the world and different people—hearing and understanding different languages. There were the mountains, oceans, and deserts to be explored!

It was a Friday morning. The Farmer's Market was in full swing, and there were people everywhere. Buyers and sellers were hustling and bustling, trying to make sales and get good bargains. But Grandma had other plans that day.

Grandma lived on the second floor of an apartment building. When I arrived, she was moving around, doing her own busy work. She drew the curtains, closed the doors, and suddenly acted very secretive.

Her son, who came only once in a while, lived in a nearby hotel. He also had his own room on her floor, but seldom occupied it. He managed to have good control over Grandma.

That morning, Grandma was different. She appeared a little nervous. First she made me sit down, but I could see her moving around in her bedroom. When she came back to the living room, she carried several stacks of money, which she had stockpiled under her mattress. I didn't know what she wanted. On the table in front of me lay $1000 worth of marks. She instructed me who was going to get it and where it was going. I was to take so much for tithing and offering for the church. The young preachers and helpers were to receive so much. But what I remember best was she handed me enough money to go to America. Grandma wanted me to go to South America, but I told her that pretty soon I was leaving for North America.

I left her place in total awe, carrying a paper sack full of money. Traveling by train, streetcar, and subway, I safely carried all the money back to the church.

1967

Preparation was in swing for a fall revival meeting. Dr. Charles Butterfield was the main speaker. He had his own quarters, but we all ate together in the dining room. This was where it all began. Dr. Butterfield asked me about becoming a staff member on a missionary medical ship sailing to the South Seas. The door to my missionary calling was wide open. Dr. Butterfield was going to be my sponsor in America.

I wasn't going to South America, but not on the missionary medical ship. I was heading first to Washington State to go to Northwest College to pursue missions.

Immigration papers take a long time to process. The law required I could not purchase my ticket until the finality of the visa. Dr. Butterfield had informed me of my departure date—Frankfurt Airport on Tuesday, March 22, 1968. I went against all odds and secured my one-way ticket to America. Dr. Butterfield and his wife Edith had departed from the USA to the Scandinavian countries for special meetings, and we were all supposed to meet in Frankfurt, Germany.

One week before my departure date I still had not received my visa. Nervousness set in and landed in my bones. The unknown was hard to deal with. What was God's plan?

Finally a letter from the embassy arrived with a note: "Come and pick up your visa with your sponsor's signature." It seemed impossible. How was I to get that signature? It would take two or more weeks to receive a signature from Northwest College. I did not know the whereabouts of my sponsor. Darkness engulfed me. My trip, my ticket, world missions all washed away? I needed a supernatural miracle. "Lord," I said, "it is up to you. It is out of my hands. I am trusting you!"

This was Thursday. I had Friday and Monday. I needed to say goodbye to my family and I still had to get to Frankfurt. I searched for the eye in the storm—my little world had almost caved in. Thursday night was prayer meeting and I sat by the phone. Why the phone? I did not know. My somber mood did not please the Lord. I seemed to have drawn into a cocoon when the phone rang.

The voice requested Christel Decker. With confidence I spoke up. The voice said, "Christel, this is Charles Butterfield. Edith and I are here in

Hamburg. Our flight was rerouted because of visibility in Copenhagen, Denmark. We were unable to land so now we are here, in your city."

It was unbelievable! Breathlessly I said, "To get my visa, I need your signature." Brother Butterfield invited me to his hotel and I had the document signed without a minute to spare.

On Saturday I traveled home for a short visit, arriving in Frankfurt on time for my flight to America. The last few weeks and months had been very stressful. All the personal luggage I had was two suitcases with my personal belongings. An overseas trunk was filled with small household items, bed linen that did not fit, and pillows that were not square like my mother's at home. My hairdryer, which did not fit in the socket, was shipped by freight, sea, and land, and was to arrive in about six to eight months.

On the plane I had a lot to think about. Mom was concerned about me traveling with total strangers to a far and distant world. She had read about the horrors of missing girls. The songwriter tells it this way:

> I traveled down a lonely road,
> And no one seemed to care.
> The burden on my weary back had bowed me to despair.
> I oft complained to Jesus how folks were treating me,
> And then I heard Him say so tenderly:
> "My feet were also weary up on the Calvary road;
> The cross became so heavy that I fell beneath the load.
> Be faithful, weary pilgrim; the morning I can see.
> Just lift your cross and follow close to me."
>
> Oh Jesus, if I die upon a foreign field someday,
> T'would be no more than love demands
> No less could I repay.
> No greater love has mortal man than for a friend to die.
> These are the words he gently spoke to me:
>
> "If just a cup of water I place within your hand,
> Then just a cup of water is all that I demand."
> But if by death to living they can thy glory see,
> I'll take my cross and follow close to thee.
> —Ira Stanphill

It was a very long flight. The weather had been quite cool in Germany. The trees still didn't have any leaves; the early spring flowers had popped their heads out, only to be nipped by night frost.

It was early in the morning when our plane touched down. Transportation was arranged to get me to Northwest College. Springtime had arrived in Seattle. There was a lovely fragrance and warm air all the way around. The magnolia trees were flowering; pink cherry trees lined the road. Everything looked magnified—the cars were much bigger, and the roads and streets were wider. Even the sun was much brighter. I needed some time to take this all in.